Improving
FORMATIVE ASSESSMENT
PRACTICE
to Empower
Student
Learning

D1401126

Dedicated to the teachers of the Rockville Centre Public Schools who have opened academic doors for all children through their firm belief in equity and excellence, and to those courageous New York principals who have resisted reducing the work of all teachers to the sum of student test scores.

Improving
FORMATIVE ASSESSMENT PRACTICE
to Empower Student Learning

E. Caroline Wylie
Arlen R. Gullickson
Katharine E. Cummings
Paula E. Egelson
Lindsay A. Noakes
Kelley M. Norman
Sally A. Veeder

Foreword by W. James Popham

CORWIN
A SAGE Company

CORWIN
A SAGE Company

FOR INFORMATION:

Corwin
A SAGE Company
2455 Teller Road
Thousand Oaks, California 91320
(800) 233-9936
Fax: (800) 417-2466
www.corwin.com

SAGE Ltd.
1 Oliver's Yard
55 City Road
London EC1Y 1SP
United Kingdom

SAGE India Pvt. Ltd.
B 1/I 1 Mohan Cooperative Industrial Area
Mathura Road, New Delhi 110 044
India

SAGE Asia-Pacific Pte. Ltd.
3 Church Street
#10-04 Samsung Hub
Singapore 049483

Acquisitions Editor: Debra Stollenwerk
Associate Editor: Desirée Bartlett
Editorial Assistant: Kimberly Greenberg
Production Editor: Amy Schroller
Copy Editor: Brenda Weight
Typesetter: C&M Digitals (P) Ltd.
Proofreader: Sue Irwin
Indexer: Maria Sosnowski
Cover Designer: Nicole Franck
Graphic Designer: Karine Hovsepian
Permissions Editor: Adele Hutchinson

Copyright © 2012 by Corwin

Printed in the United States of America

Library of Congress Cataloging-in-Publication Data

Improving formative assessment practice to empower student learning / E. Caroline Wylie . . . [et al.].

p. cm.
Includes bibliographical references and index.

ISBN 978-1-4129-9701-0 (pbk.)

1. Educational evaluation. 2. Educational tests and measurements. 3. Academic achievement. I. Wylie, E. Caroline.

LB2822.75.I52 2012
371.26—dc23   2011045907

This book is printed on acid-free paper.

FSC
www.fsc.org

MIX
Paper from
responsible sources
FSC® C014174

12 13 14 15 16 10 9 8 7 6 5 4 3 2 1

Contents

List of Web Tools

These Web Tools, along with additional materials and resources related to *Improving Formative Assessment Practice to Empower Student Learning* can be found at the following address: http://www.corwin.com/wylieformativeassessment

Foreword

FORMATIVE ASSESSMENT'S ESSENCE

W. James Popham
University of California, Los Angeles

Formative assessment works. An ever-growing gob of empirical evidence attests to the truth of this pithy proclamation. But *why* does the formative assessment process work? That is, *why* does formative assessment seem able to bring about giant jumps in students' learning?

I sometimes hear colleagues urging teachers to adopt formative assessment practices in their classrooms because "research evidence supports the effectiveness of formative assessment." Yet, while I applaud anyone who tries to get teachers to give formative assessment a try, I think those who employ a "research-ratification" rationale to promote formative assessment are making a mistake. They've got it backwards. Formative assessment works *not* because there is research evidence to support it. Instead, there is research evidence to support formative assessment because formative assessment works!

To get a proper handle on the why-it-works issue, we really must understand *the essence of formative assessment.* But to do this, we first need to comprehend what something's "essence" actually is.

Let me rewind the calendar for many decades to the days when I was an undergraduate philosophy major in a small liberal arts college. Although the orientation of my professors' approach to philosophy was definitely Aristotelian because it was a Catholic college, there were also frequent dollops of St. Thomas Aquinas tossed into our studies. If I recall, St. Thomas came into play occasionally just to "tighten up" Aristotle. I really can remember—even to the exact words employed to define it—one of the most important concepts in Aristotelian philosophy, that is, the nature of something's *essence.*

My professors pointed out that, according to Aristotle, an essence was "that which made a thing to be what it is." Something's essence, therefore, could be contrasted with its "accidents." Accidents, in Aristotle's view, were the properties of something unrelated to its essence. So, if the essence of human beings were that we are "rational animals," the accidents associated with a particular human being might be the person's height, skin color, or sense of humor.

What, then, is the essence of formative assessment? What is it that truly makes formative assessment to be what it is? In my view, the essence of formative assessment is its relentless reliance on assessment-elicited evidence of students' learning-status—for teachers to make decisions about adjusting their instruction or for students to decide about adjusting their learning tactics. Whether made by teachers or by students, those adjustment decisions won't always be correct. After all, human beings make mistakes, sometimes almost hourly. But adjustment decisions predicated on assessment *evidence* regarding students' current achievement levels will almost always be better than will adjustment decisions made by teachers or students who are proceeding without assessment evidence.

Put simply, formative assessment looks at *ends* (or outcomes) as a way of deciding whether *means* (or inputs) need to be changed. This basic ends-means model is so beguilingly simple that it may, to some, seem unworthy of much attention. Yet, the use of an ends-means model underlies much of humankind's progress over the years. Unarguably, an ends-means paradigm will make teachers' instruction better. People who guide their future actions by evaluating the outcomes of their past actions will surely be more successful than will people who don't. And this certainly applies to teachers as they make their instructional decisions.

I worry these days when I encounter proponents of formative assessment who seem to be more preoccupied with the trappings of formative assessment (that is, with its "accidents") than with its essence. For example, it surely makes sense, as you will see in the pages of this exciting seven-author book about formative assessment, to suggest that the formative assessment process will be more effective if certain teacher actions are taken. We want formative assessment to work as well as it can work because, then, students will learn as well as they can learn. The authors' four characteristics of formative assessment, for example, are definitely good things to do, as are a flock of other practical suggestions their book offers to readers.

But I've recently attended several conferences in which ardent advocates of formative assessment have described what goes on in "real-world" formatively oriented classrooms. More often than not, those descriptions have arrived in the form of video-recorded classroom scenes or, perhaps, video discussions among teachers as part of a formative assessment learning community. What I've been stunned by, however, is the absence of any attention to what I regard as formative assessment's essence. What's missing is the use of students' assessment results to make adjustment decisions about what's to be done next. What we were presented with in those videos was good stuff, the sort of stuff I'd like to see in all classrooms. But there was never an illustration—*not even one*—of formative assessment's essence.

Let me underscore my concern about this absence with a few examples from recently attended conferences. Either on video, or sometimes during teachers' oral reports, we heard about the importance in formatively oriented classrooms of teachers' communicating learning targets to students. Beyond that, we were also told how to clarify the success criteria by which students could then judge how well they were doing in reaching their learning targets. Well, explicating learning targets, along with their accompanying success criteria, are definitely good things for teachers to do. Accurately described instructional intentions will typically have a positive impact on kids' learning. But these positive payoffs can transpire in classrooms where the teachers have never even heard of formative assessment. Clarified instructional intentions, when ladled out in student-friendly lingo, will almost always help make instruction more effective. And it will help make the formative assessment process more effective too. But it's not what formative assessment's essence is.

Then there's the dividend that properly framed feedback can provide for students. Numerous videos of "formative assessment in action" highlighted teachers' skillful use of descriptive feedback. When feedback is not student comparative but, instead, helps students gauge where they are and what they should do to get where they want to be, it works wonderfully. Descriptive feedback is a hands-down winner. But descriptive feedback can be advantageously used by teachers who know naught about formative assessment. Carefully crafted descriptive feedback will improve what goes on in almost any classroom. Use of descriptive feedback can also make formative assessment more effective. But descriptive feedback is not what makes formative assessment truly tick.

Besides what seems to be a preoccupation with the trappings, not the heart, of the formative assessment process, I also see different writers trying to subdivide formative assessment into more palatable chunks. Almost every author who spins out a book about formative assessment, understandably, presents a different way of cutting up the formative assessment cake. I've done so, as have other writers. Happily, research evidence suggests that the formative assessment process is sufficiently robust that, even if used in substantially different ways, it still works. It works, that is, as long as its essence undergirds whatever subdivision scheme is being recommended. The essence of formative assessment—its preoccupation with assessment-yielded evidence regarding students' status as the stimulus for adjustment decisions—needs to be central in *any sensible* conceptualization of the formative assessment process.

In the following pages, you will encounter a gaggle of good ideas about how to make the formative assessment process purr. I was particularly taken with the authors' bent for practicality—an orientation seen throughout the book. This is not a volume intended to impress the authors' colleagues—although it should. Rather, it is a book for real-world teachers written by classroom-savvy authors who know that formative assessment is a good thing for teachers to do. The book's writers offer a ton of tangible tips for teachers about how to make formative assessment work. As you read these authors' takes on how to play the formative assessment game properly, you'll like what you're reading.

Please view all of this great advice through the prism of what makes formative assessment really work. At bottom, formative assessment succeeds because it makes us attentive to assessment evidence about what's happening to kids, and then decide what to do next based on that evidence. That's the essence of formative assessment. Everything else, you see, is just an accident.

Preface

This book guides teachers in learning about and applying formative assessment sensibly to serve student learning and improvement in teaching practices. We believe in the power of the formative assessment process as a tool to assist and empower students in learning and to encourage them in the process. While the book focuses on building teachers' skills in the use of formative assessment, most important, perhaps, it provides effective strategies for building habits that serve teaching and learning. The book centers on classroom instruction and assessment. Here we guide development and use of strategies for gathering and using information in ways that serve daily instruction and encourage strong working relationships between students and teachers and among students themselves.

We think you will find this book to be a refreshing change from the standard testing approaches of most books on assessment. We banded together to write this book because too little is written about assessment outside the realm of testing. Testing, of course, is big business, and testing companies make millions through the sale of tests for summative purposes (e.g., No Child Left Behind). Most who now want to get on the "formative assessment" bandwagon choose the use of formative testing, because such tests can be packaged and sold with curricular materials. There is little money to be made in the type of assessment we encourage, but there is real gold in student learning that results from the assessment processes we present here.

This book emerged from a 2009 national conference on student assessment practices conducted under the auspices of the Joint Committee on Standards for Educational Evaluation and supported by the National Science Foundation.[1] A major finding of the conference was the need for information and materials that are practical to use and that directly assist teachers in improving their practices. A self-evaluation guide developed for the conference by two of the authors (Cummings and Noakes), along with ideas and suggestions from practicing teachers and a teacher coach, struck a strong chord among the authors, who were conference attendees, and forms the foundation of the book.

What began as an attempt to synthesize the conference findings changed in orientation to focus on formative assessment to be used by teachers. The result is material solidly grounded in research, but focused and presented in practical, how-to terms. Our book acknowledges the importance of student testing, but does not focus on testing or the use of tests and quizzes. Rather, it focuses on building teacher skills in a variety of assessment practices that support and assist daily student learning.

We built the book as a "stool" with three legs. In the first leg, we provide a well-framed definition of formative assessment and evidence of its key role in student learning and its place in the classroom. In the second leg, we set forward characteristics of formative assessment or building blocks as tools to help you prepare to develop and hone your formative assessment skills. In the third leg, we developed our ideas in terms of a recursive model. That's a fancy way of saying that we help you follow a practical, cyclical development and learning path, adding new information so that your practice in each new cycle builds from previous efforts. Together, the characteristics from the second leg and the cyclical process from the third can serve as a guide for your practice into the future.

Who Is This Book For?

This book is a guide for teachers. If you are a teacher who seeks to improve your understanding of your students, desires to build confidence in your students, and seeks improved learning among your students, you are in our audience. If your job is to assist teachers in improving their assessment practices, this book is intended for you, too. If you are a student aspiring to be a teacher, you can gain

---

[1]This material is based on work supported by the National Science Foundation under Grant No. 0736491. Any opinions, findings, and conclusions or recommendations expressed in this material are those of the authors and do not necessarily reflect the views of the National Science Foundation.

much from this book. If you are comfortable with where you are, how you are teaching, and believe your students are learning as much as they are capable of learning, this book is not for you.

Special Features of This Book

The value of the book for your self-development efforts is substantially enhanced by four attributes:

1. Real-world examples. In each chapter, we include examples of teachers using formative assessment in their classrooms as they go through the process of changing practice. These composites from actual teachers and teaching situations add clarity to the ideas presented. They range from elementary through high school examples and a variety of subjects. We are necessarily limited in how many examples we can provide; but rest assured, even if you cannot find an example that matches your grade or subject area, the process of formative assessment will still apply to you and your students. These examples also provide specific, practical exemplars of steps teachers have taken, outcomes they have achieved, things they have learned, and improvements they have made based on their reflections. Learning communities, coaches, and administrators will find these examples useful for introducing and discussing formative assessment issues.

2. Array of online tools. We have included templates for organizing, gathering, and systematically using information to serve your formative assessment development needs. These tools are described, included in examples, and made available for your use through web-based access. The first time we mention a particular tool in a chapter, a margin icon will remind you that you can download it from the website. We encourage you to use, modify, and share these tools with other teachers.

3. Objectives and big ideas. For quick reference, we begin each chapter with a clearly stated objective and close each chapter with a summary of the big idea. This presentation method serves both to focus each chapter and to reinforce knowledge/skill development.

4. Questions. We conclude each chapter with a set of questions to help teachers, individually or in groups, think further or deeper about the chapter's main ideas. In addition to helping reinforce what has been learned, the reader is encouraged to go beyond the specific ideas presented and consider new options and opportunities.

Given the many books now available about classroom assessment practices, why should you buy and use this one? When all is said and done, this book is uniquely worthwhile in at least three ways.

- This book focuses on formative assessment as a continuous process that serves student learning—tests and quizzes get no attention, none, other than as one of many sources of evidence that teachers and students can draw on.
- This book treats teachers' skill development in formative assessment practices as a continuing process with the goal of producing sound lifetime habits. Grounded in research, it is practical in application with both how-to exemplars and practical tools made available to serve teachers' self-development.
- This book provides insights into how teachers can dramatically improve teaching effectiveness and student learning and therefore make teaching and learning more enjoyable. That perspective, if not unique, is certainly rare among books on assessment.

Chapter Highlights

The book includes seven chapters. In Chapter 1, we introduce the general concept of formative assessment in the context of student learning goals, identifying where students are in relation to those goals, and using feedback to make adjustments to instruction. In Chapter 2, we describe several common ways in which formative assessment practice is defined and applied—what it looks like in practice. In Chapters 3 and 4, we provide practical steps all teachers can take to consider and begin personal self-development efforts by determining a focus and planning for making specific formative assessment changes. In Chapter 5 we focus on practical steps to implement changes. In Chapter 6, we describe how to evaluate the changes you made using systematic processes to guide your learning and ensure that the changes made do serve students in direct and sound ways. In Chapter 7, we draw on the big ideas of all chapters to synthesize the ideas of the book and suggest avenues for moving forward with what has been learned.

We think you will find the book easy to read and filled with excellent, practical guidance for improving your skills in formative evaluation. We designed it to be used by teachers on their own or in a small learning community. The ideas, tools, and practices we included are intended to enable you to implement them without the guidance of a staff development expert. Our experience suggests you will persist and enjoy the learning process more if you engage with other like-minded teachers. Reading Chapters 1 and 7 first will give you a sense of the whole book, which might be helpful before you begin in earnest.

As you read, we believe you will say often, "I do some of this already, but I never thought of this part." Enjoy the book for its insights into classrooms, for the ways in which it builds on common classroom practices, and for its attention to tradeoffs you make when implementing new ideas. As you implement the book's ideas, share your assessment learning intentions with your students. They will appreciate knowing that you care enough to work to make your teaching the very best.

Finally, in keeping with our intention to help you grow in your assessment skills, we seek your feedback. As you read this book and apply its ideas, please note which ideas work best, what you find problematic, and what alternative strategies can apply, and let us know. This book also is a work in progress. We know that with your input it can be improved. Contact information for the authors is included in the web support materials.

Acknowledgments

A large number of people influenced and assisted us during the preparation of this book. Several have had a marked influence on materials constructed and our efforts to present them in ways that are readable and useful to teachers. Emily Rusiecki participated in developing the first draft of the *Formative Assessment Guide* and its first trial. Amy Gullickson reviewed our book and worked with us to revise several chapters extensively. Numerous teachers, administrators, and friends gave us input, advice, and information about their own formative assessment practices. These include Jeffrey Alvarez, Lauren Buckowsky, Stephen Burkholder, Angela Dick, Jordan Edwards, Stephen Henry, Alaire Long, Barbara Lutz, Jordan Kreher, Tricia McNamee, Summer Pettigrew, Donnia Richardson, Nancy Schisler, Teresa Songs, and Brandy Wilson. We have appreciated their willing assistance and support in this effort.

We note with special appreciation the extensive amount of time, effort, and assistance provided by Debra Stollenwerk, senior editor at Corwin. She helped us define, shape, and organize our book to make it relevant and useful to teachers. We believe the book is much better because of her interest and engagement with our unruly team of authors.

Publisher's Acknowledgments

Corwin gratefully acknowledges the following individuals for their guidance and editorial insight:

Nicole Cobb, Director
Center for School
   Climate
Tennessee Department of
   Education
Nashville, TN

Barbara B. Howard, Assistant
   Professor, Leadership and
   Educational Studies
Appalachian State University
Reich College of Education
Boone, NC

Joan Irwin, Professional
Development Consultant
Newark, DE

Sherry L. Markel,
Professor
Northern Arizona University
College of Education
Flagstaff, AZ

Kathleen M. McCoy, Associate
Professor
MLF Teacher College
Arizona State University
Tempe, AZ

Marianne Moore, Instructional
Specialist
Middle/Secondary
Transition
Virginia Department of
Education
Richmond, VA

Eugenia Mora-Flores, Associate
Professor
University of Southern
California
Rossier School of Education
Los Angeles, CA

Lyndon Oswald, Principal
Sandcreek Middle School
Ammon, ID

Layne Parmenter, Elementary
Principal
Uinta County School District #6
Lyman, WY

Beth Passaro, Middle Grades
Initiative/ Gear UP
coordinator
Queens College
New York, NY

Julie Prescott, Assessment
Coordinator
Vallivue High School
Caldwell, ID

Jennifer Ramamoorthi, 5th
Grade Teacher
CCSD21, Field School
Wheeling, IL

Laurie VanSteenkiste, Staff
Development Consultant
Macomb Intermediate School
District
Clinton Township, MI

Grace B. Velchansky, Elementary
Language Arts Consultant
Macomb Intermediate School
District
Clinton Township, MI

Barbara Weaver, Adjunct Faculty
School of Education
College of William and Mary
Hampton, VA

About the Authors

E. Caroline Wylie, PhD, is a Research Scientist at Educational Testing Service. She holds an under- graduate degree in applied mathematics and physics, a postgraduate certificate in teaching mathematics and information technology and a doctorate in educational assessment, all from Queen's University, Belfast.

Her current research addresses issues of the use of formative assessment to improve class- room teaching and learning. She has been involved in projects that are focused on the creation of effective, scaleable, and sustainable teacher professional development. Related research projects have focused on the formative use of diagnostic questions for classroom- based assessment, and the impact that the sustained use of such ques- tions has on classroom instruction and student learning. Current work includes an investigation of how learning progressions can be used to support formative assessment in mathematics. Several of these projects have been supported by large grants, for which she has been the principal investigator or coprincipal investigator.

Previous work at ETS includes serving as the lead ETS developer of the National Board for Professional Teaching Standards (NBPTS) certificates for middle and high school science teachers and elemen- tary school art teachers.

Arlen R. Gullickson, PhD, is Professor Emeritus at Western Michigan University. He served as The Evaluation Center director from 2002 to 2007 and as its chief of staff from 1991 to 2002. Dr. Gullickson chaired the Joint Committee on Standards for Educational Evaluation from 1998

to 2008, during which time the committee developed *The Student Evaluation Standards* (2002), revised *The Personnel Evaluation Standards, Second Edition* (2007), and was engaged in revising *The Program Evaluation Standards, Second Edition* (1994) for the third edition, published in 2010. He has worked extensively in education as a secondary math and science teacher, professor of educational research and evaluation, and in the conduct of federally funded research and evaluation projects. In 2011, he stepped down from directing an NSF-funded Advanced Technological Education evaluation resource center (EvaluATE) to become its codirector. He has received several major service awards, including the Western Michigan University's Distinguished Service Award (2002), the American Evaluation Association's Alva and Gunnar Myrdal Evaluation Practice Award (2007), and the Consortium for Research on Educational Accountability and Teacher Evaluation's Jason Millman Scholar Award (2008). Although his primary work emphasis for the past 20 years has focused on program evaluation, he maintains a strong interest in classroom evaluation practices. He has authored numerous journal articles, book chapters, and book materials. With Peter Airasian, he authored the *Teacher Self-Evaluation Tool Kit* (1997) which presaged many of the ideas presented in this book.

 **Katharine E. Cummings** earned a PhD in secondary education with an emphasis in teacher preparation at the University of Illinois in 1989. Prior to that time, she was a high school teacher and counselor in Fargo, North Dakota. Cummings directed the secondary education program at North Dakota State University before moving to Western Michigan University in 1999. She has directed the School/University Partnership Team at WMU and was co-coordinator of the CITE Collaborative with Kalamazoo Public Schools in 2002–03. Currently, Cummings serves as the Associate Dean of the College of Education and Human Development at WMU and provides technical assistance in the assessment of student learning for academic and student services programs. Her research interests include the assessment of candidates in teacher education, the use of benchmarking to build assessment skills in preservice and inservice teachers, and program evaluation in higher education. Nationally, she has served as a member of the NCATE Board of Examiners and on the Association of Teacher Educators' Commission on Teacher Induction and Retention.

Paula E. Egelson, EdD, is the Director of Leadership Research at the Southern Regional Education Board in Atlanta. She was formerly the director of the Center for Partnerships to Improve Education at the College of Charleston (SC).

    Dr. Egelson has an undergraduate degree in child development, a master's degree in reading education, and a doctorate in educational leadership. She has worked as a community organizer, a school improvement and literacy program director for a federally-funded educational lab, a K–8 classroom teacher, and as a reading specialist. Dr. Egelson has served as the principal investigator for several large literacy grants. She has a background in research and has developed teacher evaluation, literacy, high school performance assessment, class-size reduction, school improvement, and English language learners products for PreK–12 educators.

Lindsay A. Noakes is an Assessment for Learning Research Fellow at The Evaluation Center and a doctoral student in the Interdisciplinary PhD Program in Evaluation at Western Michigan University. In this capacity, she is involved with the evaluation of various educational programs in schools and communities. She is actively engaged in Assessment for Learning research and works toward helping educators implement research-based student assessment and evaluation practices in a variety of contexts. Ms. Noakes holds a master's degree in mathematics from Eastern Michigan University and has been involved in numerous educational reform projects and committees. As a classroom teacher for nearly a decade, she has worked with students in Grades 5 through 12 specializing in instruction for gifted-and-talented students. Lindsay currently focuses on work with preservice teachers.

Kelley M. Norman is a Mathematics Instructional Coach for Topeka Public Schools in Kansas. She has two undergraduate degrees in English and education and is currently working on her master's in educational administration. She has previous experience teaching fourth grade, where she was responsible for content across the curriculum. After moving up to middle school, Kelley taught sixth- and eighth-grade math. For the last four years, she has been working with middle school mathematics teachers as an instructional coach. In one of her roles as a coach, Kelley works closely with teachers to assist them in developing their formative assessments practices through collaborative meetings, observing, modeling, and analyzing student work with individual teachers or groups of teachers.

Prior to her retirement from Western Michigan University in September 2010, **Sally A. Veeder** served as Assistant Director of the WMU Evaluation Center for more than 26 years. Included in her many duties (supervising staff, serving as a member of several project staff projects, signing off on the proposals and reports developed by staff members, approving travel and other expenses, etc.) was proofreading/ editing the many proposals, reports, correspondence, and books that were developed/written by Center staff members. In addition, she collected and wrote the information/contributions of Evaluation Center staff for the bimonthly University newsletter (PRISM). She twice served as an officer of the University's Administrative Professional Association and received quarterly and annual WMU Support Staff Awards. Also, she served on the staff of the Joint Committee on Standards for Educational Evaluation during the periods that Daniel Stufflebeam and Arlen Gullickson served as the chair of that committee. Two books were written during those periods, and Ms. Veeder edited both: *The Student Evaluation Standards: How to Improve Evaluations of Students* and *The Personnel Evaluation Standards: How to Assess Systems for Evaluating Educators.*

1

Introduction to Improving Formative Assessment Practice

We consider *formative assessment* to be the continuous process in which students and teachers engage to monitor learning and to inform future instruction. The research literature identifies the consistent and careful use of formative assessment to be an important factor for improving student learning. This book is for teachers who want to know more about formative assessment and who want to improve their own practice in this area. Readers will be at different stages in their practice, some more familiar with formative assessment than others, some more proficient than others. The purpose of the book is to help all teachers examine their practice—regardless of how proficient—and to find ways to make improvements.

This book has been written so that it can be used by an individual teacher who wants to pick it up and work through the chapters. However, we recognize that there is significant value in groups of teachers working together on their practice. Therefore, the approach is such that this book also can be used by a small, informal group of teachers, a whole department, and/or coaches or mentors working with individual teachers. In short, it can be used by anyone whose goal is to improve his or her formative assessment practice.

A reflective practitioner is someone who spends time critically examining his or her practice with the goal of improving it (Schon, 1983). In a world of ever-increasing demands on teachers, finding time for analysis and self-evaluation may be difficult. For a teacher who desires to improve her practice, there is the question of how to identify an area on which to focus. Should she examine her classroom discourse practice to ensure that she is fair in terms of the types of questions and expectations that she has of boys and girls alike? Should she look at her instruction to see to what extent she uses real-world and cross-curricular contexts in her instruction? Should she focus on her assessment practices? As the title of this book suggests, we consider the examination of formative assessment practices to be a valuable, ongoing exercise for teachers. However, rather than asking you to just accept our perspective, the next chapter articulates what we mean by formative assessment and the impact it can have on student learning—which, of course, is why we consider it to be an important topic for self-reflection and ongoing improvement.

In this chapter, we make several clear distinctions important for this book: between formative and summative assessment and between assessment and evaluation. We describe how evaluation of teaching practice can be part of ongoing professional development and how this self-evaluation process will unfold as the book progresses.

Formative and Summative Assessment

To make sense of the rest of what follows in this book, it is important to be clear about the distinction between formative and summative assessment. A teacher engages in assessment in a variety of ways, as captured by the following questions: What is the mood of students as they enter the classroom? How attentive do they seem today? What do they remember about this topic from yesterday or from last week? Are students ready for the upcoming test? How can students support each other in the learning process? Which students are ready for a new challenge? Which students need another opportunity to explore the topic from a different perspective? Some of these questions might be asked as part of the formative assessment process, while others would not. For example, while it is critical that a teacher assess and pay attention to students' moods and levels of attention, those aspects are not directly parts of formative assessment. All the other questions could be asked as part of formative assessment. As noted in the introduction, we consider *formative assessment* to be a continuous process in which students and teachers engage to monitor learning and to inform future instruction. Formative assessment is an important part of instruction that has been shown to have a positive impact on student learning when used systematically and consistently.

> Formative assessment is a continuous process in which students and teachers engage to monitor learning and to inform future instruction.

By contrast, *summative assessment* is the term usually given to assessments that "sum up" learning by measuring the amount of knowledge, skills, or abilities that someone has at a particular point in time (Glickman, Gordon, & Ross-Gordon, 2009). In school contexts, these assessments can be large-scale, high-stakes assessments—that is, assessments taken by all students in a particular grade, in a district or state, under standardized circumstances. Summative assessment can also refer to the measures that contribute to end-of-course or end-of-year grades given to students. While the reach of the assessments used to determine that grade may not extend beyond a particular school, once the grade has been given, there is rarely an opportunity to further influence it. Thus, summative assessments can be thought of as static measures with generally no further instructional opportunities to shape learning. Clearly, summative assessments are not something to be ignored; however, they are not the focus of this book.

We believe that while knowledge of formative assessment is important, competence or proficiency in formative assessment practices is really our goal for each teacher reading this book. For that reason, the book is built around opportunities for you to reflect on your practice, consider alternative approaches, and put them into practice in your own classroom, so that you develop competency in formative assessment practices, not just knowledge of formative assessment. The remainder of this chapter will introduce the self-evaluation process to provide a sense of what will follow in the rest of the book.

The Purpose of the Book

This book includes opportunities for you to reflect on your formative assessment practice, consider alternative approaches, and try them in your classrooms, so you can develop not only knowledge of formative assessment characteristics but also competency in formative assessment practices.

Evaluation and Formative Assessment

In this book we use the terms *evaluation*—and often *self-evaluation*—and *formative assessment* a great deal. In many contexts, assessment and evaluation are synonymous. For example, it is equally appropriate to talk about a fitness assessment or a fitness evaluation. However, to be as clear as possible in the book, we assigned different roles and meanings to these terms. *Formative assessment*, as defined previously, refers to the continuous process in which teachers and students engage to monitor learning and make appropriate adjustments. *Evaluation*, in this context, refers to the process in which a teacher examines an aspect of practice—in this instance, to examine formative assessment practices. In this book, evaluation always focuses on the teacher's personal practices and accomplishments. For that reason, evaluation and self-evaluation are treated as synonymous. Table 1.1 illustrates how the actors, partners, and subjects differ.

| Table 1.1 | Distinguishing Between Formative Assessment and Evaluation |

	Formative Assessment	**Evaluation**
Actor	Teacher	Teacher
Partner	Students	Peers, coach, administrators
Subject	Student learning	Formative assessment practice
Purpose	Improve student learning	Improve teaching practices

As the table illustrates, formative assessment involves the teacher as the primary actor and students as partners. By contrast, while evaluation also involves the teacher as the primary actor, partners are more likely to be other adults with whom they can work, such as peer teachers, coaches, or administrators. The focus or subject of the two processes is also different. While formative assessment is focused on collecting evidence of the specifics of student learning, evaluation (in this book) is focused on the formative assessment practice itself. This distinction relates to the purpose of the two processes. Formative assessment seeks to directly improve student learning by more accurately tailoring learning opportunities to student needs. Evaluation in this context is conducted to improve teaching practices, which, in fact, then will affect student learning. While the next chapter focuses solely on formative assessment, the subsequent chapters focus more on evaluation of formative assessment practices.

Evaluation and Professional Development

In some recent writing about teacher professional development, the language shifts from the term "professional development" to "professional learning" (Darling-Hammond, Wei, Andree, Richardson, & Orphanos, 2009). We think this is an important recognition of the fact that changing teaching or formative assessment practices is an ongoing effort that requires learning and practice. More traditional professional development opportunities will have much less impact on practice.

Here our focus is on the teacher as a learner. We do not assume that teacher professional development can be guided only by external experts or prepackaged units of instruction. Rather, we assume that every school includes teachers or content coaches who have expertise in specific aspects of formative assessment or who are willing to explore and learn together. Furthermore, we believe that teachers can benefit from the expertise of their colleagues and that expertise can be developed collectively with appropriate resources and support.

This book invites you to engage in self-evaluation, plan for improvement, implement changes, and reevaluate your practice. It is based on a process of continuous improvement rather than on a series of individual training sessions. Support for continuous improvement exists close to the teacher's classroom and is not dependent on funding, release time, or external consultants. However, we firmly believe that when teachers are working in a school where collaborative time is provided or teachers have opportunities to observe each other, the improvement process is much more effective.

In using the material in this book, you will be asked to build upon your strengths and identify your weaknesses through self-evaluation. We recommend that you work with a trusted colleague or a small group of colleagues in this process. We also realize, given the busy lives of teachers, that practitioners can benefit from a structured process for their self-evaluation and development. In pilot projects using the self-evaluation tools that we describe in later chapters, we found that teachers benefited from having more guidance and structure to help them in this process. You will notice that we provide questions at the end of the chapter for you to think about on your own, but also questions that you can address with a group of peers. Working with a colleague in a community of practice strengthens the learning of the entire group.

The Self-Evaluation Process

In the chapter that follows, we describe the formative assessment process as a cycle in which a teacher is continually asking a series of three questions (Wiliam, 2004): Where are my students headed? Where are they right now? How can I close the gap between where they are and where I want them to be? The formative assessment process is all about identifying learning goals for your students and then identifying where they are in relation to those goals. The gap-closing is achieved through timely, specific, corrective feedback; adjustments to instruction; and engaging peers in the support process. While these steps move students closer to the original learning goals, they also enable the teacher to establish new goals as learning progresses.

Students engaged in formative assessment also can ask these same questions: Where am *I* headed? Where am *I* right now? How can *I* close the gap between where I am and where I want to be? The three questions also have applicability in terms of your self-evaluation of how you implement formative assessment. You can ask yourself, Where am I going? Where am I now? How do I close the gap?

The Self-Evaluation Cycle

Where am I going? (Chapter 2)

Where am I now? (Chapters 3 and 4)

How do I close the gap? (Chapters 5 and 6)

Where Am I Going?

As a teacher who is about to embark on an evaluation of your own formative assessment practice, you also can think about the three questions above in relation to your formative assessment practice. The first question is "Where am I going?" Rather than focusing on *student* learning goals, in formative assessment the focus is on *your* learning goals. In the next chapter we give you a vision of formative assessment practice. Some aspects of the descriptions are likely familiar to you and represent practices you already use in your classroom. Other practices may be less familiar to you or may not be things that you do on a regular basis.

Where Am I Now?

The second question is "Where am I now?" Chapters 3 and 4, along with the accompanying materials on the website, are designed to help you identify areas of practice to work on. This question creates a cyclical process. Thus, you likely will return to these chapters and the resources on more than one occasion as you choose different areas of practice on which to focus.

How Do I Close the Gap?

The remaining chapters are designed to support you in the exploration of formative assessment ideas to help you answer question 3, "How do I close the gap between where my current practice is and where I want it to be?" Just as the self-evaluation aspect of Chapters 3 and 4 is something that you will revisit, these final chapters are also part of that cyclical process.

The Journey

There is no *right* way to begin this process. Each person's formative assessment journey will be unique. Each of you has a distinctive profile of strengths and weaknesses. Furthermore, each of you can choose different areas of focus for new approaches in your classroom. Effective formative assessment practice is multifaceted, but you do not need to begin working on all fronts immediately. What is important is that you identify some place to start (and Chapter 3 will help you with this).

Think of this process like training for a triathlon. Many people who decide to compete in a triathlon do so because they really like to swim, run, or bike, but they are not necessarily strong in all three areas. Training is an incremental process, starting with shorter distances than the ultimate race will require, but building up gradually over time. Training in one area tends to have benefits across the other areas. Swimming is a great cardio workout, resulting in improved stamina. In turn, improved stamina benefits the running and cycling components of the race.

Improving formative assessment practice is a bit like training for a triathlon—your strength may be engaging students in peer assessment or asking questions to get at the heart of student learning. You may need more training in other areas, but you can begin the process gradually. There will be cross-training benefits. For example, suppose you choose to focus on learning intentions for each lesson to identify the key information students need. The process of working on learning intentions, perhaps with a colleague, may actually help you develop better classroom questions to identify whether students really have understood the learning intention.

Overview of the Chapters

In Chapter 2 we present two examples of formative assessment practice and then examine several different definitions of formative assessment. We also present some of the research about the impact that formative assessment can have in your classroom.

In Chapter 3 we describe the beginning point for the self-evaluation process. Here we give you an opportunity to think about the general information about formative assessment in the context of your own instructional practice. Our goal is to help you choose a target area from the full breadth of formative assessment. Establishing a more limited focus will help you with the evidence collection process we present in Chapter 4.

In Chapter 4, we focus on an in-depth evaluation of the area or areas you identified initially in Chapter 3. We suggest sources of evidence to help with this process, such as observing or informally interviewing peers. In addition, we introduce several resources that can be found on the website accompanying this book. After you have identified your own strengths and weaknesses with respect to formative assessment, we conclude Chapter 4 with setting goals and creating a specific plan to guide your actions for four to six weeks. There is no expectation that any one set of goals would represent all the changes you might ultimately want to make to practice. Rather, in Chapter 4 we focus on selecting goals that are achievable and manageable. What are you going to do to change your practice?

Chapter 5 focuses on ways in which you can find support to help you implement change, both in terms of people that can support you and actions that you can take. Chapter 5 introduces the idea of the learn-practice-reflect-revise cycle (Thompson & Wiliam, 2008). Here we invite you to try out some new practices in your classroom, reflect on them, and revise as necessary. This forms a cycle of action within the larger process, which is a cycle in and of itself. Figure 1.1 illustrates the larger cycle that is driven by the content in Chapters 3 through 6, along with the smaller cycle, which is the specific focus of Chapter 5.

Chapters 6 and 7 conclude the book with the idea of an evidence chain. This evidence chain supports you to think through the question, "How will I know if I have been successful?" It also helps you decide when you are ready for a new challenge with respect to formative assessment.

Before you begin an in-depth reading of each chapter, you might also find it helpful to read Chapter 7. This chapter provides a summary of the big ideas in this book. Knowing the end point might help you better plan your journey to get there.

Figure 1.1 The Cycle-Within-the-Cycle Process

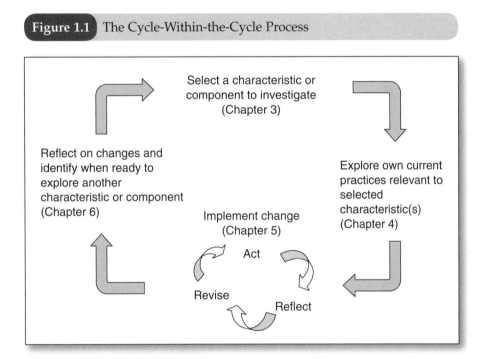

Figure 1.1 will be used at the start of Chapters 3 through 6 to reorient you to where you are in the process. The next chapter is your opportunity to examine formative assessment more closely, beginning with two examples of practice. It is an exciting journey, and we wish you well with it as you begin.

2

Examining Formative Assessment

The purpose of this chapter is to give you an overview of formative assessment. First we present two examples of teachers who are using formative assessment. You may have some questions as you read through these examples, but you will probably recognize the teachers' intentions and actions even if you do not have a strong understanding of formative assessment. Following the examples and the brief discussions about the ways in which they are similar and different, we examine several different definitions of formative assessment to tease out critical aspects of this process. We then briefly review some of the research about the impact of formative assessment on student learning. Finally, we present four characteristics of formative assessment that we use in subsequent chapters and that you will use as you plan to implement formative assessment in your own practice.

Formative Assessment in Practice

In this section, we illustrate the use of formative assessment through two examples of how teachers implemented formative assessment with their students. The examples provide snapshots of what these teachers do, but the examples do not reflect the full breadth of their practice. We deliberately have not provided a great deal of contextual information, but rather want you to focus on how teachers and students engaged in the formative assessment process. To that end, each example concludes with some commentary about what they did, and the section concludes with some comparisons and contrasts between the two examples.

First Example of Formative Assessment

In this example, a teacher engaged in a formative assessment process in which her actions were transparent to her students. She was partway through an economics unit on international trade. As students came in the classroom, the teacher directed them to a question posted on the board that addressed a major idea covered in several previous lessons. Students were familiar with the routine of starting a lesson with an "entrance ticket" or ending the lesson with a brief question that each student answered individually as their "exit ticket" to leave the class. The teacher used student responses to these entrance or exit tickets to inform her instruction to the current or subsequent lesson. Responses were not used as part of the grading process.

In this instance, students individually wrote their responses on Post-it© notes and took them up to stick on the board. Students did not put their names on their responses. Once everyone had responded, the teacher reviewed each response and engaged the whole class in a discussion about how well each response addressed the question. Responses were then classified by the students into three categories: "correct," "almost there," or "not quite." The majority of the responses fell in the "not quite" category. After the review was complete, the teacher asked the class, "So what does this tell me?" Several students mumbled things like "we don't get it yet" or "we're stupid"; and the teacher quickly interrupted those responses and said, "No! It gives me information to help me decide what to do next. And I think I need to have you complete one more activity to help you understand this concept a little better before we are ready to move on."

Several important aspects of formative assessment are evident in this teacher's practice. The teacher began this lesson with a very specific question in mind: Were students ready to move on to the next part of the unit or did she need to spend additional time reinforcing the concept that they had been working on? She made her purpose very clear to the students: they were not being graded on their responses, and the exercise was entirely to inform the teacher. In addition, the teacher had come to the lesson prepared to either continue with the unit as planned or to complete an additional activity to reinforce the concept if it turned out that students were still struggling. Furthermore, she clearly expressed her attitude that it was her responsibility to ensure that students had sufficient learning opportunities, rather than suggesting that it was the students' fault that they had not yet learned this particular concept.

The teacher in this example used the opening question in class to help her decide the best possible use of the class time to meet students' learning needs. She conveyed to students where they currently were in their learning with respect to the goals she had articulated for them and provided an additional learning opportunity to deepen their understanding. In terms of the formative assessment cycle, this teacher was able to identify a learning gap between where she wanted students to go and where they were, and she was prepared to provide additional instruction to help close the gap.

A Second Example of Formative Assessment

In the next example, the teacher brought her fifth-grade students directly into the formative assessment process. In a series of lessons, the students had been learning to write a persuasive essay, and they had just completed a first draft of their conclusions. They previously had talked about the elements of a quality conclusion. In the observed lesson, the teacher had selected a couple of conclusions from students in the class and made copies (without students' names). Students were divided into small groups. She assigned each group a specific element and asked them to discuss how well each selected conclusion met the element and to determine specific feedback for the conclusion writer.

After groups had time to discuss the examples, the teacher worked with the whole class, showing each conclusion on the overhead projector. Groups in turn reported on their discussions and provided their feedback. Several groups of students began their feedback by identifying what was strong about the particular example before moving on to provide feedback for improvement.

The writers of each conclusion remained anonymous but the teacher indicated that she would provide a copy of the feedback to the students after class. In the subsequent lesson, students had an opportunity to work on their own or with a partner to review their own conclusions, to think about the kinds of feedback that had been discussed the previous day, and to make revisions.

This example illustrates different aspects of formative assessment. The value of reviewing and providing detailed feedback on the three conclusions extended significantly beyond the three students. All students had an opportunity to examine student writing products against the elements of a quality conclusion and to think about how to make each one better. A notable feature of this observed lesson was that students were clearly comfortable with work from classmates being used as exemplars.

The teacher had clear learning goals for this class and had already provided success criteria for students (the elements of a quality conclusion). By providing students with an opportunity to evaluate other students' writing against those characteristics, they were then more prepared to evaluate their own writing against the characteristics. By listening to the feedback from the students, both in the small groups and as a large group, the teacher also was able to collect evidence about how well the students understood the elements of a quality conclusion or whether they needed some additional support to apply them.

Comparing and Contrasting the Two Examples of Formative Assessment

In both examples, the formative assessment process was used to guide what happened next in the classroom. In the first example, based on student responses, the teacher decided what activity was needed next. In the second example, students took the feedback they received from their peers to make changes to their writing. In both examples, student work was shared freely to support the learning process. The teachers accomplished this either by sharing student responses for review by the rest of the class or by using specific examples of student work for students to practice using the rubric to provide feedback. In both instances, the teachers protected students' privacy by using anonymous examples, thus supporting a safe classroom environment.

The two examples also provide a contrast in terms of who led the action. In the economics example, the teacher directed the collection of evidence of student learning, via her entrance ticket question, and led a discussion of student responses. In the writing example, the teacher set the stage by providing examples of student work to be critiqued. Students had the more central role in organizing and presenting information, and they directly provided feedback to their peers.

The more prominent role of students in the second example is a shift for some teachers, who see their role as the primary providers of feedback to students. However, when teachers train students to understand the nature of appropriate and inappropriate feedback and provide them rubrics or exemplars, students can provide valuable feedback to one another. In addition, students benefit from the process of providing feedback themselves. They become more aware of the demands of the task and learn to recognize stronger and weaker responses.

Understanding Formative Assessment

An important starting point for the journey to examine your formative assessment practice is to be clear on exactly what formative assessment means. In this section we present several definitions to help you develop—or deepen—your understanding of formative assessment. While there is a broad consensus on the idea of formative assessment, each definition has a slightly different nuance, which will help you refine your understanding.

Black, Harrison, Lee, Marshall, and Wiliam (2003) described formative assessment as occurring when "information about learning is *evoked* and then *used* to modify the teaching and learning activities in which teachers and students are engaged [emphasis in the original]" (p. 122). The Council of Chief State School Officers (CCSSO, 2008) defined formative assessment as "a process used by teachers and students during instruction that provides feedback to adjust ongoing teaching and learning to improve students' achievement of intended instructional outcomes" (p. 3). Popham (2008) presented a similar definition: "Formative assessment is a planned process in which assessment-elicited evidence of students' status is used by teachers to adjust their ongoing instructional procedures or by students to adjust the current learning tactics" (p. 6). One of this book's authors along with colleagues defined the overarching principle of formative assessment as "Students and teachers using evidence of learning to adapt teaching and learning to meet immediate learning needs minute-to-minute and day-by-day" (Educational Testing Service, 2009, p.5).

Complementary Definitions of Formative Assessment Emphasize Different Aspects of Practice

Emphasizing Feedback:

"A process used by teachers and students during instruction that provides feedback to adjust ongoing teaching and learning to improve students' achievement of intended instructional outcomes." (Council of Chief State School Officers, 2008, p. 3)

Emphasizing the Time Frame:

"Students and teachers using evidence of learning to adapt teaching and learning to meet immediate learning needs minute-to-minute and day-by-day." (Educational Testing Service, 2009, p. 5)

Emphasizing Planning:

"Formative assessment is a planned process in which assessment-elicited evidence of students' status is used by teachers to adjust their ongoing instructional procedures or by students to adjust the current learning tactics." (Popham, 2008, p. 6)

Emphasizing Instructional Modifications:

"Formative assessment occurs when information about learning is *evoked* and then *used* to modify the teaching and learning activities in which teachers and students are engaged [emphasis in the original]." (Black, Harrison, Lee, Marshall, & Wiliam, 2003, p. 122)

It can be helpful to look across these various definitions because different aspects of the practice are emphasized in each, as noted in the call-out box. There is significant agreement across these definitions of formative assessment, in large part due to the fact that each was developed with the same research basis for formative assessment in mind. The extensive review of published research on formative assessment conducted by Black and Wiliam (1998), along with other work, such as that of Brookhart (2005) and Nyquist (2003), illustrate a strong, positive connection between teachers' use of formative assessment in everyday teaching and improved student learning.

From the definitions presented in the call-out box, it should be clear that formative assessment is tightly connected to what happens "in the moment" of teaching. The ETS definition has the most explicit reference to time, but all the definitions suggest that to meaningfully influence the teaching and learning in a classroom, formative assessment must happen more frequently than just quarterly or monthly. Thus, the continuous and ongoing nature of formative assessment is evident. Popham's (2008) definition emphasized the role of planning in formative assessment. Sometimes it may occur spontaneously, but for formative assessment to be truly effective, anticipating and pre-empting student misconceptions or difficulties is important. In other words, while formative assessment will happen "during instruction," significant planning and preparation needs to occur separately from instruction. All the definitions include the words *adjust, adapt,* or *use* with respect to the collected evidence; in other words, collected evidence that is not then used is of no formative value.

Deeper Than Just a Definition of Formative Assessment

The previous definitions provide a starting point, but it is worthwhile to look more deeply at these various perspectives to clarify both what is formative assessment and what is not. For these purposes, we explore in more detail both the CCSSO and Black and Wiliam perspectives to better define the domain of formative assessment. In addition, we return to the formative assessment cycle introduced in Chapter 1. As you will see, this cycle is another way to think about formative assessment, but it builds upon the ideas inherent in the CCSSO and Black and Wiliam perspectives.

The CCSSO clarified and expanded its definition through five attributes (McManus & CCSSO, 2008): learning progressions, learning goals, specific feedback, collaboration, and self- and peer assessment. Most of the attributes closely align with the definitions of other groups presented previously. Learning progression, however, is an attribute not well attended to by others.

Most definitions or explanations of formative assessment acknowledge the importance of presenting clear learning intentions to students. The CCSSO work, however, pushed further, recognizing the need for individual lesson-level learning intentions to be connected in meaningful sequences of learning, or learning progressions. This emphasis suggests the importance of coherent instruction over longer periods of time as an important foundation for meaningful formative assessment. The interested reader can find further explanation of the CCSSO definition and attributes in McManus and CCSSO (2008).

Based on Black and Wiliam's (1998) research, ETS (2009) divided formative assessment into five key strategies:

1. Clarifying and sharing learning intentions and criteria for success

2. Engineering effective classroom discussions, questions, and learning tasks that elicit evidence of learning

3. Providing feedback that moves learning forward

4. Activating students as owners of their own learning

5. Activating students as instructional resources for one another

The first three strategies focus primarily (although not exclusively) on the teacher's role. First, the teacher is the primary person who will set direction for learning through learning intentions and criteria for success. Learning intentions or learning goals form a critical map for teachers: (a) to illustrate what kinds of learning are important prerequisites for new knowledge and skills, (b) to guide the determination of the current level of learning, and (c) to indicate where learning should be headed.

Second, the teacher engineers questions, discussions, and tasks so that learning toward the particular goals can be evidenced. Discussions, questions, and learning tasks all provide opportunities to collect evidence of student learning. It is critical that teachers have enough time and supporting resources to engineer these events to ensure that they get the precise information they need.

Third, the teacher provides feedback to help students achieve those goals. To make an impact on future instruction, teachers often have to make instructional adjustments. One such adjustment is feedback to students to help them see where they are in their learning and to nudge them along to the next stage.

The final two of the five Black and Wiliam strategies focus on students' roles in terms of reflecting on their own learning and supporting the learning of their peers. Engaging students in this way can increase the number of learning and feedback opportunities. Often, the process of providing thoughtful and appropriate feedback to peers helps students learn to evaluate and reflect on their own learning. Note that even in these two strategies, teachers play a crucial role in activating students' ability to be reflective through careful structure, guidance, and modeling.

The formative assessment cycle we present in this book is compatible with both the ideas and positions inherent in both the CCSSO- and the Black and Wiliam–based strategies. This cycle includes three parts, or phases: collecting, analyzing, and using evidence to inform instruction. We chose this cycle perspective because of its focus on continuity. Plus, we have found this three-phase division of formative assessment useful for teachers, since the challenges of each phase are different. Wiliam (2004) noted that "in order for assessment to function formatively, it needs to identify where learners are in their learning, where they are going, and how to get there" (p. 5). Although roles and responsibilities differ, teachers and students alike need to (a) know where learning is intended to go; (b) have ways of identifying students' current position with respect to those goals; and, most importantly, (c) make use of the assessment information to help close the gap between current position and desired goals.

All the definitions we have presented focus on the roles of teachers and students because the audience for formative assessment is narrower than that of other assessment types. Ultimately, the purpose of formative assessment is to inform instruction for a particular lesson or set of lessons and for a particular group of students. Thus, the primary audience necessarily is limited to that teacher and those students.

> **The Formative Assessment Cycle**
>
> Where are students headed?
>
> Where are they currently?
>
> How do I close the gap?

> **Further Reading**
>
> For further reading, there are several helpful reviews of formative assessment: Andrade & Cizek, 2010; Heritage, 2010; Popham, 2008

The Impact of Formative Assessment on Learning

In the previous section, we mentioned that the various literature reviews indicated that there was a strong, positive connection between teachers' use of formative assessment in everyday teaching and improved student learning. We discuss that further in this section to provide encouragement. We believe strongly that your efforts to develop and deepen your formative assessment practices will be worth it.

There is a robust literature base for the impact of formative assessment on student learning, with several notable reviews of the literature for formative assessment and formative feedback: Black and Wiliam, 1998; Brookhart, 2005; Crooks, 1988; Hattie, 2009; Hattie and Timperley,

2007; and Natriello, 1987. The authors identified experimental studies that showed a positive impact on student learning for various aspects of formative assessment as well as other teaching behaviors. Through these studies, formative assessment practices, alone and in combination with other teaching techniques, emerge as the most potent of teaching techniques for producing and supporting student learning.

While literature reviews are powerful for establishing and documenting causes, individual studies often provide more insight into practical applications of methods. For that reason, we have included several individual studies in the call-out box here. Each study listed in the box includes a control group—in other words, some randomly assigned teachers who continued "business as usual"—while other teachers (the treatment group) made changes to their practice according to the focus of the study. This kind of study allows the researchers to conclude that the outcome (positive or negative) the treatment group experiences can be attributed to the specific change they made and is not just because of different students, curriculum, and so on.

Further Reading

The following experimental studies support specific aspects of formative assessment:

- Providing students with clear learning intentions as a foundational base—Fuchs, Fuchs, Karns, Hamlett, Dutka, & Katzaroff, 2000; White & Frederiksen, 1998
- Using effective questions, tasks, and discussions to elicit evidence of learning—Bergan, Sladeczek, & Schwarz, 1991; Carpenter, Fennema, Peterson, Chiang, & Loef, 1989
- Supporting student learning through the use of formative feedback—Butler, 1987, 1988; Day & Cordon, 1993; Kluger & DeNisi, 1996; Simmons & Cope, 1993
- The roles of students in the assessment process, both to reflect on their own learning and to support peers through the use of feedback on peers' work—Fontana & Fernandes, 1994; King, 1992; Mercer, Wegerif, & Dawes, 1999

Typically, both individual studies and literature reviews show the potency of strategies through use of what is termed *effect size*. An effect size is a statistical way of comparing results of two groups by calculating the standardized mean difference between the two groups. An effect size of zero (0) means the strategy had no effect. A positive number such as 0.3 means the strategy was effective; an effect of 0.6 would be twice as effective. Of course, a negative number would mean the strategy made things worse.

For example, a follow-up set of studies to the Black and Wiliam (1998) review, focused on mathematics and science teachers who participated in professional development on formative assessment (Wiliam, Lee, Harrison & Black, 2004), resulted in a positive impact on student learning with an average effect size of 0.32. Those student learning effects resulted from teachers' individual efforts over a year's time to build and use sound formative assessment practices in their classrooms. We think studies such as these are important because they unambiguously demonstrate that, as teachers develop their formative assessment skills, students accrue the benefits.

Formative Assessment Characteristics Used in This Book

As summarized previously, formative assessment has been defined in a variety of ways, each consistent with the overall research on formative assessment, but each providing slightly different insights into the concept. In this book, we use four characteristics to help you tease apart the various aspects of formative assessment as you look at your instructional practice. The four characteristics include:

1. Intended outcomes of learning and assessment are clearly stated and shared with students.

2. Formative assessment opportunities are designed to collect quality evidence that informs teaching and improves learning.

3. Formative feedback to improve learning is provided to each student.

4. Students are engaged in the assessment process and, to the extent possible, in planning their own next steps for learning.

On the website associated with this book, you can download the *Formative Assessment Guide*. This resource presents the four characteristics and components of each characteristic, along with examples of each component in practice and guiding questions to support reflection on each characteristic. The remainder of this chapter will elaborate on critical aspects of each of the four characteristics. On the following page is an excerpt of the *Formative Assessment Guide* that illustrates how the *Guide* presents the characteristic, related components, and guiding questions: in this example we have shown the first characteristic.

FORMATIVE ASSESSMENT CHARACTERISTIC #1

Intended outcomes of learning are clearly stated and shared

Component	Example of Component in Practice	Focus Questions to Guide Discussion
(a) Clear Learning Expectations	Teachers base learning expectations on a thoughtful analysis of relevant standards (state, district, national, etc.), curriculum guides, student needs, previous learning, and overall trajectory of intended learning. Teachers share explicit learning expectations (both long term and daily) with students using understandable language.	How do you utilize multiple sources of learning expectations? How do you determine when specific learning expectations should be addressed? How do you ensure that shared learning expectations are written using student-friendly language? How do you know that students understand the learning expectations?
(b) Clear Success Criteria	Teachers openly discuss success criteria or expectations for performance with students. Teachers align success criteria with learning expectations. Teachers share rubrics and exemplars with students to illustrate performance expectations. Students and teachers have a shared understanding of quality.	How do you provide students with rubrics/ performance guidelines? How do you know that students understand the success criteria? How are students able to give input and feedback on success criteria? How do you know your students share your understanding of quality?

Stating and sharing intended outcomes of learning and assessment, the Guide's first characteristic, is really the foundation for all formative assessment activities. This characteristic includes two components: learning expectations and success criteria. Learning expectations, or learning goals, are used to articulate what students will learn in a lesson.

Success criteria describe how students will demonstrate that they have learned what was intended (see the call-out box for examples of learning expectations and success criteria). Both learning expectations and success criteria should be shared with students in a way they can understand. Though it is implicit in the characteristic, we note explicitly that success criteria are directly aligned with learning expectations. Further, this characteristic calls on teachers to develop a shared understanding of quality work and performance guidelines with students.

Learning Expectations and Success Criteria

Learning expectations and success criteria work together to help teachers and students understand what is to be learned and what evidence will demonstrate that learning has taken place. For example,

Learning expectation: students will understand the components needed to create a simple circuit.

Success criterion: students will be able to draw or create a simple circuit.

Learning expectation: students will understand the conventions of a business letter.

Success criterion: students will be able to list three ways that a business letter differs from a letter to a friend.

Learning expectation: students will understand how to use descriptive language to evoke a sense of time and place in fictional writing.

Success criterion: students will be able to revise drafts of current stories to incorporate at least three examples of descriptive language.

In each of the examples above, the learning expectation is stated as what the student will know or understand, not what they will be able to do. The demonstration of the knowledge is the heart of the success criteria: how will you and your students know that the learning intention has been achieved?

The second characteristic is that formative assessment opportunities are designed to collect quality evidence that informs teaching and improves learning. This characteristic focuses on the primary goal of any formative assessment: to inform the teaching process and improve learning. Formative assessment can be used to determine student needs, monitor student progress, and modify instruction as necessary. Formative assessment can be used at the start of a new unit to gauge students' prior knowledge and understanding and throughout each lesson, enabling students to use assessment information to improve their learning. Even summative assessments provide opportunities for students and teachers to be more informed about strengths and weaknesses, which can inform future teaching and learning. When this approach is used, assessment is presented to students as a continuous process for individual improvement with many and varied opportunities to demonstrate their knowledge and skill.

The two examples of formative assessment presented at the very beginning of this chapter illustrate this characteristic, focusing on the role of formative assessment during instruction. In the first example, the economics teacher used the evidence of student learning collected from the entrance ticket to directly influence how the remainder of the time for that lesson would be spent. In the second example, the language arts teacher structured the lesson so that students' feedback informed their revision process. As the teacher listened to their comments, she was provided with information that allowed her to determine if any intervention or reteaching with an individual student, a small group, or the whole class was necessary.

The third characteristic is that formative feedback to improve learning is provided to each student. In other words, students are provided with ongoing, relevant feedback to help them gauge learning progress and improve performance. The feedback provided is clearly aligned with learning expectations and is specific to individual student needs. Royce Sadler (1989) described feedback as information that is provided to students that they can use "to alter the gap" between their current position and the learning outcome they are aiming for (p. 121). In other words, feedback is not telling students

Ways to Give Students Written Feedback

Direct a student back to the rubric to check that he or she has addressed all the elements of the project.

Ask an open-ended question to help move student thinking along.

Identify specific responses that are incorrect and suggest that the student work with a partner to review those questions.

Comment on one or two strengths of the work along with an area of focus for improvement.

Remember, if you are going to take the time to write feedback that helps students focus on one or two critical areas for improvement, then students need to have the opportunity to use that feedback.

what the correct answer is, but instead giving them enough information to help them advance their learning.

When writing feedback (or planning what to say for oral feedback), teachers are scaffolding information for students who perhaps do not yet fully understand either the learning goal or the success criteria. The feedback should help them understand what they have done that matches the success criteria and what does not. Feedback should help them think about the next steps they can take. Most important, students need an opportunity to actually *use* the feedback. In other words, if feedback is given when a project or task is completed, there is little (probably no) opportunity for students to make use of that information. Feedback needs to be provided before the project or task has been completed so that students can learn from it and improve their work. Feedback can take many forms, such as these:

- a description of how student work does and does not match the success criteria or rubric, which directs a student back to the rubric (or specific aspects of it) to check that he or she has addressed all the elements of the project
- asking an open-ended question to help move a student's thinking along
- identifying some responses that are not correct and suggesting that the student work with a partner to review those questions
- commenting on one or two strengths of the work, along with an area of focus for improvement

Feedback is:

- Helping students understand what they did that matched the intended learning and what did not.
- Support provided to students that helps them move forward in their learning.
- Given to students as soon as possible.
- Provided at a point in instruction when it can make a difference.

Feedback is NOT:

- A grade or a score with no explanation. A grade is usually summative and suggests no opportunity to improve.
- A grade or a score with some additional explanation. Research shows that students will focus on the grade and either decide they can live with the grade

(Continued)

(Continued)

and don't need to do more work or are upset by the grade and don't want to focus on the additional feedback.

- An explanation with no opportunity to incorporate the information into another draft. If students don't have an opportunity to use the feedback, it was time wasted writing it.

The final characteristic of formative assessment is that students are engaged in the assessment process and, to the extent possible, in planning their own next steps for learning. This characteristic encompasses both student self-assessment and peer assessment. Too often, formative assessment is considered only in terms of the teacher role, ignoring the student role. We believe that students should be placed at the center of assessment by actively and regularly participating in the assessment process. Students are guided through the self- and peer-assessment process so they are able to provide quality feedback to themselves and others. We have found that students often benefit by first engaging in peer assessment before self-assessment. It is often easier for them to learn to use a rubric or other descriptions of success criteria when looking at a peer's work than when looking at their own work. An important aspect of this characteristic, much like formative feedback, is that some kind of action needs to be taken after the assessment itself. Students might act on their own self-assessment information, teachers might use that information to support the students' learning, or students might need time to incorporate the feedback from peers into their work.

In the language arts example provided at the beginning of the chapter, the roles of both peer and self-assessment were demonstrated. Peers first worked in small groups to provide feedback on conclusions written by other students in the class, using the characteristics of a quality conclusion that they had previously discussed. Reviewing this feedback as an entire class gave students a way to better understand these qualities. The students then had an opportunity to engage in self-assessment by reviewing their own conclusions against these same qualities or in peer assessment by reviewing them with another student.

This section introduced the four characteristics of formative assessment used in this book. In Table 2.1, the characteristics are further broken down into two or more components. The table also provides some examples of how each component would play out in practice. As you examine this table, you can review the previous narrative descriptions of each characteristic to see how each component was addressed in those descriptions.

| **Table 2.1** | Formative Assessment Characteristics and Components With Examples of Practice |

Component	*Example of Component in Practice*
CHARACTERISTIC #1: *Intended outcomes of learning are clearly stated and shared* Teachers share learning expectations (what students will learn in a lesson) and success criteria (how they will demonstrate that they have learned it) with students in a way that students can understand. Success criteria are directly aligned with learning expectations. Students and teachers develop a shared understanding of quality work and performance guidelines.	
(a) Clear Learning Expectations	Teachers base learning expectations on a thoughtful analysis of relevant standards (state, district, national, etc.), curriculum guides, student needs, previous learning, and overall trajectory of intended learning. Teachers share explicit learning expectations (both long term and daily) with students using understandable language.
(b) Clear Success Criteria	Teachers openly discuss success criteria or expectations for performance with students. Teachers align success criteria with learning expectations. Teachers share rubrics and exemplars with students to illustrate performance expectations. Students and teachers have a shared understanding of quality.
CHARACTERISTIC #2: *Formative assessment opportunities are designed to collect quality evidence that informs teaching and improves learning* The primary goal of any formative assessment is to inform the teaching process and improve learning. Teachers develop and share assessments with colleagues and use these assessments throughout the lesson to determine student needs, monitor student progress, and modify instruction as necessary. Teachers present assessment as a continuous process for individual improvement with many and varied opportunities for students to demonstrate their knowledge and skill. Students use assessment information to improve learning.	
(a) Formative Assessment at the Launch of Learning	Teachers gather information (informal and formal preassessments) at the start of each lesson, unit, or topic to determine student prior knowledge and interest in the subject. Teachers use the results of the preassessments to inform the instructional design to meet the needs of students—e.g., some topics might only need review, some might need more in-depth instruction, some assume prerequisite knowledge might need to be taught.

(Continued)

(Continued)

(b) Formative Assessment While Guiding Students Through Learning Experiences	Teachers align formative assessments with learning expectations and use them continually throughout units of study to inform revisions of instructional plans. Teachers use formative assessments to systematically monitor whole class and individual student progress. Teachers individualize formative assessments to meet the needs of students.
(c) Formative Assessment While Checking for Understanding	Teachers use summative assessments formatively to determine the need for remediation and/or enrichment and confirm learning progressions (student readiness). Teachers provide students with multiple opportunities to demonstrate learning progress by using a variety of assessment strategies that allow for student choice and continued revision.
(d) Assessment Quality	Teachers develop and evaluate assessments collaboratively to ensure quality and appropriateness of use. Assessments are appropriate for the intended purpose.

CHARACTERISTIC #3: *Formative feedback to improve learning is provided to each student*

Teachers provide students with ongoing, relevant feedback (separate from grades) to help them gauge learning progress and improve performance. Teachers align feedback with learning expectations and make sure that feedback is specific to individual student needs. The feedback reflects the teacher's understanding of contextual factors as well as learning expectations.

(a) Appropriate Feedback	Feedback is relevant to the educational task and aligned with learning expectations. Feedback is specific and clear and refers to specific learning objectives and skills rather than to student behaviors. When providing feedback on assessments, teachers identify strengths along with areas for improvement. Teachers individualize feedback based on student needs.
(b) Feedback Use	Feedback is corrective in nature and helps redirect student learning. Students are given the opportunity to revise and edit their work. Teachers provide regular feedback to students in a timely manner so that it can be used. Teachers provide students with time, opportunity, and a clear structure for using feedback. Feedback is nonjudgmental in nature to encourage learning.

CHARACTERISTIC #4: *Students are engaged in the assessment process and, to the extent possible, in planning their own next steps for learning*

Students are at the center of assessment and actively and regularly participate in the assessment process. Teachers guide students through the self- and peer assessment process so they are able to provide quality feedback to themselves and others.

(a) Student Self-Assessment	Students are familiar with a variety of self-evaluation techniques and are expected to use these techniques frequently. Students understand how to provide themselves with quality feedback and make changes to their own work. Teachers monitor students' self-assessment and provide additional instruction or support as necessary.
(b) Student Peer Assessment	Students are instructed in ways to provide appropriate peer feedback and are guided through the feedback process. Peer assessments are used only formatively and are never the basis for summative conclusions or grades.
(c) Follow-Through	Students are part of conversations about their own learning. Teachers and students discuss assessment information together and make a plan for remedial and/or enrichment activities. Students are held accountable for the execution of their learning plans.

In the next chapter, we concentrate on how you can identify an initial area for focus on your formative assessment self-evaluation. We begin that chapter with a suggestion that you might want to reread this chapter—or the classroom examples—a second time before moving forward. We also encourage you to review the *Formative Assessment Guide* available on the web to become comfortable with the characteristics (listed above) and components of formative assessment that further explain each characteristic.

Summary: The Big Idea of Chapter 2

Formative assessment is a process for both students and teachers that begins with creating a shared understanding of the learning goals between both parties. In addition, it is important that both teachers and students use a variety of approaches to get information about the current learning status for individual students. This information should be gathered frequently and then used to adjust instruction. Adjustments can take the form of feedback, peer support, and/or new or adapted instruction. We presented four characteristics of formative assessment and will continue to refer to them in future chapters.

Questions for Individual Consideration

1) What grabbed your attention in Chapter 2? Did this chapter challenge or support your thinking about formative assessment? If so, how?

2) Consider a single lesson from your most recent day of instruction. What aspects of that lesson can you connect to one or more of the four formative assessment characteristics?

3) With which of the four characteristics are you most comfortable or familiar? Why?

Question for Consideration as a Learning Community

1) As members of the group share some of their responses to the questions above, what do you notice? Are there common themes?

3

Getting Started on Your Self-Evaluation Journey

As we alluded to in Chapter 1, the process of self-evaluating your formative assessment practice will be a cyclical one. In this process, you will start by closely examining some aspect of formative assessment practice and, within that narrower focus, identifying potential areas for change or growth. As those changes first become familiar and then habitual instructional routines, you can then select another area of practice on which to focus. However, getting started can seem a little daunting. The purpose of this chapter is to walk you through those first steps. In the visual representation of the process in Figure 3.1, walking through the first step means we will focus on the gray box highlighted in the cycle.

Beginning the Self-Evaluation Process

The first step in self-evaluating your formative assessment practices is to select an area on which to focus. Although you can pick any one of the four characteristics (or components within a characteristic) presented in Chapter 2 and listed in the next box, it is worth taking a little time to make a considered selection. This chapter contains some ideas to think about in this selection process. The great thing about

Figure 3.1   The Cycle-Within-the-Cycle Process: Narrowing Your Focus

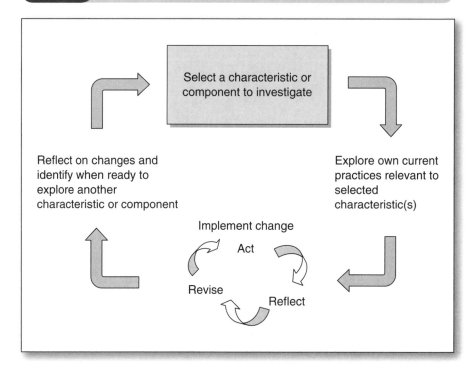

this first step is that there are many options since each teacher is an individual with varying strengths and weaknesses, interests and contexts. Provided that you stay within the topic of formative assessment, guided by the four characteristics, you will be just fine. And remember, although you have to select one thing on which to focus as your starting point, you will have further opportunities to review other areas as you continue the self-evaluation cycle.

Four Characteristics of Formative Assessment

Intended outcomes of learning and assessment are clearly stated and shared with students

(a) Clear learning expectations
(b) Clear success criteria

Formative assessment opportunities are designed to collect quality evidence that informs teaching and improves learning

(a) Formative assessment at the launch of learning
(b) Formative assessment while guiding students through learning experiences

(c) Formative assessment while checking for understanding
(d) Assessment quality

Formative feedback to improve learning is provided to each student

(a) Appropriate feedback
(b) Feedback use

Students are engaged in the assessment process and, to the extent possible, in planning their own next steps for learning

(a) Student self-assessment
(b) Student peer assessment
(c) Follow-through

Developing Familiarity With Formative Assessment

Is the topic of formative assessment relatively new to you? If so, before selecting an area on which to focus, it will be helpful to review the characteristics of formative assessment to help organize your thinking about your practice. Even if you have recently read Chapter 2, you might want to reread it with an eye now to thinking about an area to investigate in your own practice. You might view the chapter a little differently the second time around. To help you further your understanding of formative assessment, we have included references to additional resources throughout Chapter 2.

We encourage you to read the specific examples of how various teachers in different subject areas and grade levels enacted formative assessment in their classrooms. Remember, each example does not describe their entire practice, just one or two aspects of it. Think about how your teaching context is similar or different—and how that particular example of practice might play out in your classroom. In addition, the online *Formative Assessment Guide* (Web Tool A) has a series of questions associated with each component that provide another way to examine your own practice.

In this section, we address three distinct ways that you might expand your own knowledge of formative assessment and your understanding of how your current practice lines up with what is described in the research literature. On the website associated with the book, there is the *Formative Assessment Practices Survey*, which we describe following. A second source of help comes from your colleagues. Finally, we describe how reflection on your current practice can support your developing understanding.

The Formative Assessment Practices Survey

The companion website for this book includes a *Formative Assessment Practices Survey* (Web Tool B) for you to print out, with questions designed to step you through specific practices associated with each of the four characteristics presented in Chapter 2. The survey is not an extensive set of questions; you can complete it in a relatively short time. For each practice, you will be asked to think about your instructional practice and rate it from "I don't do this at all" to "I am proficient at this and could mentor others." Unless you choose to share your results with a colleague, no one will see these responses, so be candid. If one of the questions does not make sense to you, flag it as something that you might want to explore further. Each question, regardless of how you respond to it, is another tool to help you think about the nature of formative assessment. In Figure 3.2, we present a teacher's responses to the survey to show you how the survey looks. Following the figure are two examples of how two teachers (Tracy and Jason) used the survey. You will learn more about Tracy and Jason in Chapter 5.

Figure 3.2 An Excerpt of Tracy's Survey

Component Level Categories	Survey Statements	I do not do this at all	I am developing skills in this area	I am proficient in this area	I could mentor another in this area
Concurrent With Learning	Formative assessments are used to systematically monitor whole class and individual student progress		X		
	Formative assessments are individualized to meet the needs of students	X			
Formative Assessment at the Close of Learning	Summative assessments are used formatively to determine need for remediation, enrichment, and confirm learning progressions		X		
	Students are provided with the opportunity to demonstrate learning progress by using a variety of assessment strategies that allow for student choice and continued revision			X	

Formative Assessment Theme #3					
Appropriate Feedback	Feedback is relevant to the educational task and aligned with learning expectations	X			
	Feedback is specific and clear and refers to specific learning objectives and skills rather than to student behaviors	X			
	When providing feedback on assessments, strengths are identified along with areas of improvement	X			
	Feedback is individualized based on student needs	X			
Feedback Use	Feedback is corrective in nature and helps redirect student learning	X			
	Students are given the opportunity to revise and edit their work		X		
	Regular feedback is provided to students in a timely manner so that it can be used	X			
	Students are provided with time and a clear structure for using feedback	X			
	Feedback is nonjudgmental in nature to encourage rather than discourage learning	X			

Two Teachers' Responses to Completing the *Formative Assessment Practices Survey*

Tracy completed the *Formative Assessment Practices Survey* and then looked at patterns in her responses. She noted that she already had some knowledge in several aspects of formative assessment practice. She regularly determined learning objectives from district curriculum, state standards, and the curriculum resources. She shared these learning objectives with students by posting them on a board in her classroom and also by telling students the learning goals for that day. She regularly used the end-of-learning or unit summative assessments to determine areas for remediation. One area where she thought she had room for growth was in the kinds of feedback given to students. She had not previously thought about the fact that the only feedback she provided to students was in the form of graded work. Reading

(Continued)

(Continued)

more about each of the four formative assessment characteristics, she saw multiple ways to give students feedback during instruction; however, she decided she would need to learn more before being ready to try out any changes.

Jason was a beginning science teacher at a Title I middle school. He was continually frustrated by the fact that students were not performing well on his end-of-unit assessments. When filling out the *Formative Assessment Practices Survey*, he had identified five or six areas where he thought he needed to improve his practice. This seemed overwhelming to do all at once. He decided to begin with just a single area: incorporating small, formative assessments at key points throughout the course of teaching a unit and using these to monitor student progress. He realized that a good next step might be to talk with other teachers in his department to see if they could collaborate on identifying key concepts and assessments to go with each major component of the unit.

Take some time to download the survey from the website, complete it, and then return to this chapter. Once you complete the survey, review the pattern of your responses. Is there a characteristic where your practice is stronger or where you have gaps in your practice? Do you think you might want to start on a characteristic where you already have some success or in an area where you have not previously had so much experience? Does one strike you as being more challenging or less challenging than another? Perhaps as you read the examples of formative assessment in practice, you thought, "I do that!" or "That's a bit like something I do," or "I've never even thought about doing that." Jot some of these ideas down in the space at the end of the survey.

Using Your Colleagues

The second source of information that you can easily access are your own colleagues. Too often, the practice of teaching is done in relative isolation; there is always the audience of students, but rarely other teachers. Even when teachers gather together, conversation can focus on the struggles with a particular student or class, an upcoming school event, or the school's new online report card system, for example. Less often do teachers talk about their own craft, exchange ideas about how to explain a difficult concept to students, discuss common student misconceptions that might emerge during the next unit of instruction, or brainstorm about how to help students have a more sophisticated understanding of the content. However, if you total the years of teaching practice in your department or grade-level team, you might discover a great source of experience and expertise exists for you to mine.

Depending on the culture and climate of your school, how you talk with your colleagues will vary. You might introduce the topic of formative assessment as something you can talk about in department or team meetings, talk with colleagues individually, or perhaps form a small study group of colleagues who want to explore formative assessment along with you. The *Formative Assessment Practices Survey* mentioned previously can provide you with specific things to talk about. You may also consider using the four characteristics presented in Chapter 2 as a way to structure conversation. Choosing to focus on an area of formative assessment that is already part of a colleague's practice can be a good starting point. We will talk more in Chapter 4 about how you can use an expert teacher to help you in your self-evaluation journey.

Personal Reflection

Personal reflection is a third approach to help you understand how your current practice lines up with what is recommended in the research literature and to identify a way to begin moving forward (Schon, 1983). We suggest three areas on which to reflect. First, use the definitions and characteristics of formative assessment as a lens through which to view your practice. Second, consider your students' previous experiences with formative assessment. Third, consider your specific teaching context and how it might influence choices you will make.

Aligning Practice With Definitions of Formative Assessment

In the next call-out box, we repeat four of the definitions of formative assessment presented in Chapter 2. It can be helpful to think about your own formative assessment practices in the light of these definitions by asking yourself the following questions:

- Are the formative assessment practices that I use really about formative assessment, or are they instead about good instruction more generally, or even about classroom management?
- Can I identify feedback in my own examples or connect the collection of information about student learning directly to how I plan for instruction?

- Is there a short time lapse between the collection of information and the use of it?
- Are students engaged in the process?

While not every example of formative assessment practice will result in an affirmative to each of these questions, if none of them results in a "yes," reconsider whether the practice really constitutes formative assessment. This kind of realization, in turn, can provide a great starting point for moving your own learning forward.

Complementary Definitions of Formative Assessment Emphasize Different Aspects of Practice

Emphasizing Feedback:

"A process used by teachers and students during instruction that provides feedback to adjust ongoing teaching and learning to improve students' achievement of intended instructional outcomes." (Council of Chief State School Officers, 2008, p. 3)

Emphasizing the Time Frame:

"Students and teachers using evidence of learning to adapt teaching and learning to meet immediate learning needs minute-to-minute and day-by-day." (Educational Testing Service, 2009, p. 5)

Emphasizing Planning:

"Formative assessment is a planned process in which assessment-elicited evidence of students' status is used by teachers to adjust their ongoing instructional procedures or by students to adjust the current learning tactics." (Popham, 2008, p. 6)

Emphasizing Instructional Modifications:

"Formative assessment occurs when information about learning is *evoked* and then *used* to modify the teaching and learning activities in which teachers and students are engaged [emphasis in the original]." (Black, Harrison, Lee, Marshall, & Wiliam, 2003, p. 122)

In the next box, we provide an example of a teacher's reflection on her practice. The teacher compares the details of a specific formative assessment practice against the definitions of formative assessment presented in Chapter 2. In so doing, she gains a different perspective on the nature of the practice.

One Teacher's Personal Reflection on Her Formative Assessment Practice

A mathematics teacher reflecting on her classroom practice considered how she had students respond on individual whiteboards to the warm-up questions at the start of each lesson. She thought this practice was a good example of formative assessment for two reasons. First, the warm-up questions were always related to the mathematics topics the class was studying. Second, they helped get the students settled at the start of each lesson because she made sure that each table group kept the whiteboards close at hand, the students knew the routine for starting each lesson, and it saved them from having to find scrap paper each morning.

When this teacher reflected on this practice in light of the definitions of formative assessment, she realized that she had focused primarily on the classroom management aspects of the warm-up, ignoring the wealth of information about student learning available from it. In other words, she was not maximizing how she used the evidence of student understanding to immediately inform instruction. Her usual routine was to call on a student to give the answer. If it was correct, she would ask students if anyone had answered incorrectly; however, students rarely volunteered that information. She realized that if she had students hold up the whiteboards for her to see all the responses, she would have a much better sense of which concepts students understood and with which ones they struggled. She discovered that there was a great deal she could do to improve how she began each lesson—and how she could better support student learning. Moving forward, she first wanted to see if any of her colleagues were more adept at using evidence of student learning to immediately influence instruction.

Reflecting on Your Students

A second important aspect of reflecting on your own practice is to consider your students. Ask yourself questions about your students' previous experiences, including these:

- What, if any, previous experience have my students had with formative assessment?
- Have they had opportunities to work in groups?
- Have they used rubrics to evaluate their own work or the work of their peers?
- Have they been asked to reflect on what they have learned in a lesson?

These questions are important since responses to them will suggest how much scaffolding students might need if these ideas are relatively new. New ideas for students may need to be introduced gradually, with supports or modeling. These procedures help students understand the purpose behind the idea and the steps they need to follow. Changing your teaching practice might also require changes to student practice, as the elementary science teacher in the example in the next call-out box discovered.

Scaffolding Student Experiences: "A Great Wrong Answer"

An elementary teacher was beginning to pay more attention to student misconceptions in science. She wanted to check specifically whether students had misconceptions so that she could address them in subsequent instruction. She thought about potential misconceptions and how she might address them as she planned her instruction. As she questioned students during class discussions, she attempted to elicit more about how they thought about the concepts and the misunderstandings they brought with them. Upon reflection, she realized that students were hesitant to give an opinion, suggest an idea, or provide an explanation that might turn out to be incorrect. To address misconceptions successfully, she needed to change students' perceptions of what was expected when having a class discussion. The teacher decided that a way to do that would be to give the students encouragement to respond more openly in class, so that she could learn more about what they understood or did not understand. So, for the next couple of weeks when a student gave an incorrect—or partially correct—answer or idea, she made a conscious effort to acknowledge it as "a great wrong answer." She would then add comments like, "and I'll bet if you are thinking that way, so are others in the class, so you just gave me a wonderful opportunity to help everyone." Gradually, her students became less reluctant to explain their thinking and realized that the teacher valued all thinking—even incorrect thinking. That, in turn, helped her adapt her subsequent instruction once she identified the presence of student confusions. This formative assessment practice was successful because the teacher realized that to address misconceptions in science, she needed to do more than just develop better questions to ask in class. First, she had to work on how students responded to class discussions.

As you think about what changes might begin to appear in your classroom, or what different approaches your students might see you use, consider whether or how you will explain the changes to them. Letting your students know that you are engaged in learning a new skill or set of skills can be a revelation to students and a very concrete way for you to demonstrate that learning is indeed a lifelong skill. If classroom routines are going to change, it is important to let students know about the changes along the way so they are not confused. For example, suddenly introducing wait time into classroom discussions could be unsettling for students if they don't understand what you are trying to achieve.

Reflecting on Context

A third important aspect of reflecting on your own practice is coupled to your specific teaching context. Consider how making changes to your formative assessment practice can affect your situation. Conversely, your teaching situation may affect your ability to change your formative assessment practices. For example, do you have one class that might be easier to use as a "lab" for trying out new ideas? Perhaps you have a better rapport with those students or they seem more likely to use your ideas. For self-contained classrooms, is there a content area in which you feel most confident teaching? Selecting the appropriate class or the appropriate content area to begin with can make a positive difference for you in terms of improving your skills in formative assessment.

Getting started is often a challenge, so here are some suggestions. Some areas of formative assessment practice might seem more daunting than others. If that is the case, initially you might want to select an area of focus that seems manageable, given other commitments. Or you may consider one area as intriguing or a challenge. You might decide to begin working in an area where you know your students already have some experience. For example, perhaps your fifth-grade students have not had the opportunity to do much peer assessment with you, but you know that their fourth-grade teacher used peer assessment on a regular basis. You might decide that would be a good starting point for you since the students will have some familiarity with the concepts. On the other hand, you might have been thinking already about how to improve the feedback you provide to students, so you want to start there. Or perhaps you remember that a colleague has been talking about articulating learning intentions for students more clearly. If you were to work on that characteristic, you would have someone to work with you. Perhaps you relish the challenge of working with your high school students to collect more ongoing evidence of learning rather than relying on the quizzes that you administer at the end of each unit. How each person makes the initial selection of where to start will be unique.

Am I Ready to Engage in This Process?

Remember the triathlon metaphor that we shared in Chapter 1? All this thinking about where to start can seem daunting after a while. It is important to step back and remember that this is a process. As you practice one area, it will get easier and require less conscious thought, at which point you will be ready to evaluate the impact (see Chapter 6) and add a new challenge to the mix. How you begin your "training" is a personal decision for you to make; this section will provide some suggestions for a realistic way to start.

We believe it is a personal decision about where to start this process of investigating your formative assessment practice. Therefore, it is difficult for us to provide guidelines about how you will know if you have made an appropriate choice. As you reflect on these first three chapters, think about what you already know and do in terms of formative assessment, your personal interests and context, and the resources you have to draw on. Presuming that you have now chosen a formative assessment practice focus, you are ready to move on to Chapter 4 and focus on ways to examine your selected area in more depth. In Chapter 4, we provide an overview of the various tools at your disposal that are on the website accompanying this book. The reflection questions at the end of the chapter provide a way for you to put some of your thoughts and plans in writing, which might be useful for you to refer to again later.

Summary: The Big Idea of Chapter 3

In this chapter, we presented three distinct ways that you might expand your own knowledge of formative assessment and your understanding of how your current practice lines up with what is described in the research literature. To select a starting point, you might work through the *Formative Assessment Practices Survey* as a way of thinking about your practice. You might talk with colleagues to learn more about what they do, and why. Finally, you might reflect on your practice in a variety of ways: using the components as a lens, thinking about students' previous experiences, or considering your specific teaching context. The end goal of this chapter is for you to identify an area of focus to examine your practice in much more detail (the focus of Chapter 4). The entire self-evaluation process is cyclical, so you may come back to this point repeatedly as you prepare to take on new challenges.

Questions for Individual Consideration

1) As you review your responses to the *Formative Assessment Practices Survey*, what do you notice? Are there some patterns? What areas of strength do you have, and what are the areas in which you can improve?

2) Are there colleagues in your department or grade team that you think would be role models for you as you develop or deepen your formative

assessment practice? Are there colleagues who would like to explore this area with you?

3) As you think about the various definitions of formative assessment that were presented, what comes to mind in terms of your own formative assessment practice?

4) What has been your students' previous exposure to formative assessment? Do you need to scaffold their learning?

5) How might your teaching context—subject area, age of students, previous experiences of students, school culture/climate—affect how you select an initial area of focus?

6) What characteristic—or components—will you select as you move forward into Chapter 4?

Questions for Consideration as a Learning Community

1) As each member of the group shares some responses to the questions above, what do you notice? Are there group strengths that could be shared?

2) How can you work together to support each other's learning about, and implementation of, formative assessment?

3) What support from others in the school would be helpful? Department chair, principal, others?

4) As you share responses to Question 6 above, is at least one other of you interested in working on the same characteristic or components? Might you be able to work together to share ideas and progress?

5) As you hear the characteristics or components that others have shared, do you have any experiences that you could share to help them?

4

A Targeted Look at One Area

In previous chapters, you have had the opportunity to explore the ways in which formative assessment can be implemented in the classroom and its potential benefits for you and your students. You also have selected one characteristic as a starting point for your work with formative assessment practices. In this chapter, we provide a process for a more focused self-evaluation based on the characteristic you have chosen. Using the steps presented in this chapter, you will build upon your strengths, identify potential areas for improvement, and develop a plan to implement some new practices in your classroom. Using the visual representation of Figure 4.1, the chapter will focus on the gray box highlighted in the cycle.

The process that we recommend has two distinct aspects. We describe them sequentially, although you might move back and forth between the two, rather than follow an entirely linear process. First, we describe how you can use self-reflection on your own practice and provide you with some specific tools for this task. These tools are available on the associated website for this book. Second, we describe how you can get additional data to inform your thinking from three sources: interviews with colleagues, classroom observations, and document review.

Figure 4.1   The Cycle-Within-the-Cycle Process: In-Depth Self-Evaluation

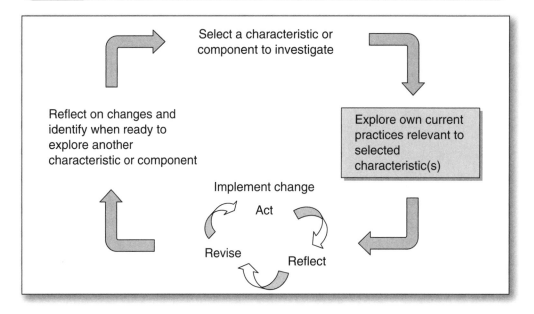

Personal Reflection on Strengths and Areas for Improvement

Most teachers are familiar with the concept of asking students to engage in a certain degree of self-evaluation by comparing their performances with the stated objectives of learning, monitoring their own progress using charts or portfolios, and planning some next steps for improvement. Students, of course, need the support and structure provided by the teacher to help them evaluate their own progress. Teachers also engage in informal self-evaluation every day when comparing class progress with plans and determining the extent to which students have met learning goals.

In this chapter, we focus on self-reflection—not of students' progress—but of your formative assessment practices. Because this kind of reflection might be a little different from what you are used to, we suggest a somewhat more formal process. The processes presented in this chapter provide the structure to help you focus your self-evaluation activities on formative assessment and its impact on student performance.

In the previous chapter, you began the self-evaluation process, one aspect of which was the completion of a questionnaire related to your assessment practices. Now, it is time to look more closely at the specific characteristic you selected and to identify the practices you are already using. Two documents, the *Formative Assessment Guide* and the *Self-Evaluation Record,* are available in this book's associated website to assist you in the process. Together, the two documents serve your initial planning needs and assist you over time as you engage in developing your formative assessment skills.

As its name suggests, the *Formative Assessment Guide* provides directions and assistance for teachers who engage in efforts to improve their formative assessment skills. The *Guide* contains a summary of the four key characteristics of formative assessment, descriptions of the components of each characteristic, and examples of the characteristics in practice. It also provides a set of questions for each characteristic to help you examine your own practices or discuss classroom assessment practices with your colleagues.

The *Self-Evaluation Record's* purpose is to help you identify and consider key issues and document and track your self-evaluation process. It also helps you organize your formative assessment efforts and information, and facilitates sharing your ideas and practices with your learning community members or supervisor. It includes four sections: initial self-reflection, collecting evidence of practice, making a plan to implement new practice, and self-reflection after implementing a new practice. Each section has one or more questions or prompts for consideration. Additionally, the *Record* provides space for taking notes and maintaining a journal of the self-evaluation process, including any questions you encounter or results you find.

Two forms of the *Self-Evaluation Record* are provided for your use. One is annotated to provide additional explanation—a help to see how the *Record* can be used. The other is blank for your immediate use.

Website Information

Take a minute, go to the website at www.corwin.com/wylieformativeassessment, and download the *Formative Assessment Guide* (Web Tool A) and *Self-Evaluation Record* for reference. You will want to print a blank copy of the *Record* (Web Tool C2) for your own formative assessment development work. We suggest you also download the annotated version (Web Tool C1) with notes for how to complete each section, and the full *Self-Evaluation Record* for Susan (Web Tool C3). The annotated version will help you get off to a quick start using the *Record*.

To illustrate how the *Formative Assessment Guide* and the *Self-Evaluation Record* can be used, we focus on one teacher, Susan. She is an 11th-grade U.S. history teacher. When she completed Chapter 3, she had completed the *Formative Assessment Practices Survey* and had taken time to do some of the suggested additional reading on formative assessment. At that point, she felt comfortable with her understanding of formative assessment and had a sense of her own strengths and weaknesses. She was ready to select a specific focus for her own development work. In the pages that follow, we examine what Susan discovered about her formative assessment practice as she worked through the self-evaluation process and collected additional evidence from outside sources.

Susan turned to the *Formative Assessment Guide* to choose a point of focus for her work. She reviewed the *Guide's* descriptions of the four characteristics of formative assessment, its examples of these characteristics in action, and the questions it posed related to each of the characteristics. She quickly realized that the *Guide* provided a well-structured way for her to think about her formative assessment focus. Figure 4.2 below gives an example of that structure. It is an excerpt from the *Guide* that identifies two distinct aspects or components of Characteristic 1 along with several examples of practice for each.

Figure 4.2   Formative Assessment Characteristic 1

FORMATIVE ASSESSMENT CHARACTERISTIC #1

Intended Outcomes of Learning and Assessment Are Clearly Stated and Shared

Teachers share learning expectations (what students will learn in a lesson) and success criteria (how they will demonstrate that they have learned it) with students in a way that students can understand. Success criteria are directly aligned with learning expectations. Students and teachers develop a shared understanding of quality work and performance guidelines.

Components	Example of Component in Practice	Focus Questions to Guide Discussion
(a) Clear Learning Expectations	Teachers base learning expectations on a thoughtful analysis of relevant standards (state, district, national, etc.), curriculum guides, student needs, previous learning, and overall trajectory of intended learning. Teachers share explicit learning expectations (both long-term and daily) with students, using understandable language.	How do you use multiple sources of learning expectations? How do you determine when specific learning expectations should be addressed? How do you ensure that shared learning expectations are written using student-friendly language? How do you know that students understand the learning expectations?

(b) Clear Success Criteria	Teachers openly discuss success criteria or expectations for performance with students.	How are students provided with rubrics/performance guidelines?
	Teachers align success criteria with learning expectations.	How do we know that students understand the success criteria?
	Teachers share rubrics and exemplars with students to illustrate performance expectations.	How are students able to give input and feedback on success criteria?
	Students and teachers have a shared understanding of quality.	How do we know that students and teachers have a shared understanding of quality?

Based on the *Guide's* materials and what she had learned from her completion of the *Formative Assessment Practices Survey* and her reading about formative assessment, Susan chose to focus on the *Guide's* Characteristic 1: "Intended outcomes of learning and assessment are clearly stated and shared with students." Using the *Guide* as an aid, she reflected on her own practice and listed things that she was already doing in her classroom to share the "intended outcomes" of a lesson with students. Her initial list of current practices is presented in Figure 4.3.

Figure 4.3 Susan's Initial Reflection of Her Practice for Characteristic 1

I write the lesson objective on the board before every lesson.

I start lessons with an "advance organizer" to embed the lesson in the larger goals of the class (only when starting a new unit).

She then used the *Guide* to serve two primary purposes. First she used it to analyze how she developed the learning outcomes she provided to the students. Second, she used it to determine whether the advance organizers she noted previously helped students understand the learning expectations for each lesson or only identified major themes in the unit.

The *Guide* also made her think about how she determined learning outcomes and expectations. She knew she had been taking the lesson objective directly from the pacing guides prescribed by her district. Due to the district prescription, Susan believed that she had very little control over the daily learning outcomes for her students. However, she now considered that even if she couldn't make changes in the stated outcomes, she could probably think of ways to help the students better understand those outcomes. One strategy she considered was finding a way to (a) word outcomes in student-friendly language and (b) get student feedback on them. She made a note of that idea, but decided that the second component of Characteristic 1 would be a better place to begin her self-evaluation.

The second component of Characteristic 1 is clear success criteria. The questions guiding Susan's evaluation of this component led her to examine the rubrics and examples she provided to her students. She realized immediately that while she sometimes had a rubric that she used when assigning a grade to student work, she had not shared it with students. At this point, she turned to the *Teacher Self-Evaluation Record* as a means to organize her thinking and manage the self-evaluation process. As you can see in Figure 4.4, Susan noted her responses to each question for the second component of Characteristic 1 using the *Self-Evaluation Record*.

Figure 4.4   Excerpt 1 From Susan's *Self-Evaluation Record*

Teacher Self-Evaluation Record

Teacher Name: Susan B. **Content Area:** U.S. History

Step 1: Initial Self-Evaluation

Characteristic	1. Intended outcomes of learning and assessment are clearly stated and shared
Component	(b) Clear Success Criteria
What might this look like in practice?	• Teachers openly discuss success criteria or expectations for performance with students. • Teachers align success criteria with learning expectations. • Teachers share rubrics and exemplars with students to illustrate performance expectations. • Students and teachers have a shared understanding of quality.

My self-reflection of this component	*I give students a description of each assignment as well as how many points the assignment is worth. They can ask me questions about it if they have any. I have specific criteria that I use when grading, but this is not shared with students ahead of time. I don't specifically "align" my assignments to the learning expectations, but I know they cover the material I am teaching. I typically don't share examples with students unless they ask. Students know what quality is when they get their grades. Overall, I don't do this very well.*
What evidence supports my self-reflection?	*On some assignments (such as big writing assignments or projects), I often find that many students don't complete the assignment the way I wanted. I thought that they should all be able to do the assignment, but many students seemed to struggle. For example, on my last research paper, the average grade was only 70 out of 100. Since this was a really big assignment, I have had to give opportunities for extra credit to make up the points. I don't really understand why they didn't know how to do the assignment because none of them asked questions about it.*
Concerns regarding practices	*I fear that giving too much structure or guidance on assignments will limit individuality and creativity in what students produce.*

We encourage you to use this *Self-Evaluation Record* for your own focus. As you complete the *Record,* list the practices you currently use on a regular basis as well as practices that you use rarely or never. You also may want to note concerns you may have about a specific practice. For example, sometimes teachers are concerned that giving rubrics to students will result in "merely filling in the blanks" in an assignment. Susan was concerned that providing detailed rubrics might actually hinder student creativity on assignments. Because the goal of this self-evaluation process is to implement improved practices in your classroom, you should address those concerns as you move through the process. Recording your concerns and reviewing your notes during application helps you to remember and return to these important matters.

After considering the questions and examples from the *Formative Assessment Guide,* your *Self-Evaluation Record* might now reference practices you listed earlier, along with some questions about whether your practices match those in the table. You have probably listed some ideas for new practices and maybe some notes about practices you are not yet ready to modify. Note the parallels between your learning process and your expectations for students. You are engaging in this self-evaluation process as a way of getting prepared for new learning. We anticipate that you are proceeding in the same way you might ask your students to "unpack" their prior knowledge and experience before beginning a new unit.

Collecting Evidence of Practice

As illustrated in the previous example, you use the *Self-Evaluation Record* to guide your collection and organization of data. We noted earlier that it is divided into four sections: "Initial Self-Reflection," "Collecting Evidence of Practice," "Making a Plan to Implement New Practice," and "Self-Reflection After Implementing a New Practice." So far, we have talked only about the first section—the initial self-reflection. In this section, we discuss what you can do to move beyond that initial self-reflection to a more systematic approach for collecting evidence of practice.

In your initial self-reflection, you considered and made notes about your current practices. Perhaps you also considered other practices that may be unfamiliar to you or that you do not use regularly. The next step in self-evaluation calls for you to use your notes as the basis for observation and discussion with your peers. This stage in the process supports you to go beyond reflection of your own practice and to examine evidence of practice from others. The second section of the *Self-Evaluation Record*—"Collecting Evidence of Practice"—serves this next step. It guides you in collecting evidence of practice from three sources of information: interviewing colleagues, observing colleagues, and document review. Each is discussed later in this section.

Before you apply your self-reflection notes to guide your collection of evidence, select one or more colleagues who can serve as exemplars. Some exemplars are teachers who are known for their ability to engage students, accomplish learning goals, and are excellent teachers. Other exemplars have strengths in specific areas of interest to you, even if there are some inconsistencies or weaknesses in their overall practice. These colleagues can serve as resources for you in your improvement process.

In choosing exemplars, consider teachers who are experienced in incorporating formative assessment practice into their everyday teaching routines. Recommendations made by peers, supervisors, students, and parents also will yield names of colleagues to consider. If other teachers in your building are going through this self-evaluation process with you, results from the self-evaluation survey (as discussed in Chapter 3) could help identify someone who is using a particular practice. If you are working with a coach, that person will help you with the identification process.

Because you will want to observe the teachers and discuss your plans with them, try to locate exemplars who work in your building. Keep in mind that you are not limited to identifying just one exemplar. Do not hesitate to learn from as many others as time will allow.

Once you have identified one or more exemplars, decide on the best way to examine his or her practices. In some cases, you can learn about your exemplar's practices through an interview or discussion. In other cases, you may choose to examine assessment documents or directly observe teaching practices. We will consider the interview process first because it may be simpler to arrange and may result in an observation as follow-up.

Interviewing Colleagues

For some formative assessment practices, interviewing a colleague may provide as much or more information than a classroom observation. Some aspects of the formative assessment process cannot be observed during the lesson. These aspects include, for example, planning the teacher might do outside of the actual lesson or his or her considerations about the evidence of student learning. Of course, you will want to find teachers who are willing and able to talk about their own practice. Some truly exemplary classroom teachers are either not comfortable talking about their practice or may be unable to identify the specific practices they use.

In our case example, Susan identified Mary as an exemplar in sharing success criteria with students. Susan had seen a rubric that Mary created for her students for their final history project last year. Mary's rubric was far more detailed than the one that Susan gave to her own students, and Mary's students seemed to produce better projects. Because Mary had previously shared her rubric, Susan initiated a follow-up discussion. Susan asked Mary to meet with her during their shared planning time to discuss rubrics. At first, Mary seemed surprised by the request, but Susan explained that she was working to improve her own assessment practices and that she valued the expertise Mary had demonstrated.

Interviewing a colleague may seem a little uncomfortable at first. After all, you probably do not often think of yourself as an "interview subject," or as an "interviewer," for that matter. However, you can ease any discomfort by clarifying the purpose of the interview and assuring your colleagues that you are not expecting them to provide a blueprint for your practice. Instead, the interview provides an opportunity for input from them regarding instructional strategies or approaches they have used effectively. From these discussions, you can consider whether those strategies are likely to fit within your own teaching or how they might be adapted to work for your students.

We recommend scheduling an interview during a time when both you and your exemplar teacher are available and when you can arrange for a degree of privacy. Trying to conduct an interview in the teachers' workroom during a noisy lunch hour is probably not going to result in clarity for anyone. Shared planning time, if available, is ideal for meeting and talking about teaching strategies. If shared planning time is not available, it is sometimes possible to schedule a before- or after-school meeting time. Some schools have provided part of a professional development day for teachers to schedule meetings.

Once the interview has been scheduled, you will want to think about specific questions you might ask your colleague. You can start by personalizing relevant discussion questions on the *Formative Assessment Guide* to fit your specific characteristic of interest. Once you have a list of questions, we suggest giving them to your colleague in advance to allow him or her to do some thinking on them before your interview.

You also may want to explain to your colleague that you will be taking notes for your own use during the interview. Recording the interview is also an option, but recordings present at least two problems. First, many teachers are hesitant to say things "on the record," especially when talking about weaknesses as well as strengths. A second problem posed by recordings is simply the time it takes to listen to them—in effect, doubling the amount of time needed for the interview (the actual interview *plus* the time needed to listen to the recorded version). It is probably more reasonable to simply take notes during the discussion and follow up if your notes are not clear. Once you have completed the interview, take time to update your notes on the *Self-Evaluation Record*. Susan's interview notes are shown in Figure 4.5.

Observing Colleagues

In addition to interviews, observations of your exemplar in action might provide you with a great deal of information about specific teaching practices. Obviously, practical concerns, such as

| Figure 4.5 | Excerpt 2 From Susan's Self-Evaluation |

Teacher Self-Evaluation Record

Teacher Name: Susan B. **Content Area:** U.S. History

Step 2: Collecting Evidence of Practice

Who seems to be an exemplar in this area? Why?	*Mary. She has shown me examples of her students' research projects, and they all do really well on the assignment.*
Interview Record (Date/ Time/Place)	*Monday, November 4, 4:45–5:25, Mary's classroom*
Interview Notes:	• How do you provide students with rubrics/performance guidelines? *Mary gives out a detailed rubric for each part of her big research paper and other projects. Smaller assignments have a standard rubric that she shares at the beginning of the year and uses throughout the year.* • How do you know that students understand the success criteria? *Mary goes over each part of the rubric with students in class. She discusses and explains each section of the rubric and students ask questions.* • How are students able to give input and feedback on success criteria? *Students can comment on whether they think the assignment is fair, but most of the feedback comes at the end when Mary looks at their completed work. That is the best indication of whether the criteria were clear and fair. If all the students didn't do well, Mary questions whether the assignment was explained clearly. Sometimes she has the students develop their own rubrics for certain assignments.* • How do you know that students share your understanding of quality? *Mary shows example student work to the students. They use the rubrics to determine the quality of the work. When their expectations are way off from hers, she gives them specific rationale.*

teaching times, might limit your ability to observe directly. Do not be too quick to rule out observations just because your planning time will not allow you to sit in on a whole class. Many administrators will help you find a way to observe a portion, if not all, of a class if it will help you. Videotaping a colleague's class will work as well.

Before the observation, think through your purpose for observing and how you will relate to the teacher you plan to observe. Identify which specific aspects of the lesson you want to concentrate on. Talk with the teacher you will observe to let that person know your focus of attention. You may want to emphasize that you are looking at specific strategies and are not trying to evaluate or judge his or her teaching as a whole. Explain that you are trying to build your own skills by carefully observing colleagues who demonstrate the skills and strategies that you want to learn. You may find that your colleagues are interested in observing you to learn from your areas of expertise as well.

Susan followed up her interview by arranging to observe on a day when Mary was going to introduce a rubric for a written assignment. Susan and Mary discussed in advance specific aspects of the class as the focus for the observation, and Susan noted them in her *Self-Evaluation Record*, as shown in Figure 4.6.

Figure 4.6   Excerpt 3 From Susan's *Self-Evaluation Record*

Teacher Self-Evaluation Record

Teacher Name: Susan B. **Content Area:** U.S. History

Step 2: Collecting Evidence of Practice (Continued)

Observation Record	Wednesday, November 13, 1:15 -1:45, AP History
What are some things to keep in mind while I am observing?	– Watch for the language Mary uses in describing the rubric to the students. Does she emphasize the points assigned for each item, or does she emphasize the process? – How do her students react? Do they work with Mary to modify the rubric in any way, or is the rubric presented as a final draft? – How does Mary show the connections among the rubric, the assignment, and the overall learning goals for the class or unit?

Using the questions she wrote, Susan took notes during the observation. She and Mary agreed to meet later in the day to talk about what Susan had observed and to discuss any questions that came up during the observation. Notice that Susan's notes focus on how Mary uses rubrics and aspects of rubric use that will help her in her own development and use of rubrics for formative assessment purposes. She does not focus on Mary's general teaching practices.

Document Review

The materials that teachers use in daily instruction often contain a wealth of information for formative assessment purposes. We encourage you to look at a variety of written documents being used by your colleagues. Depending on the characteristic you choose for your self-evaluation process, consider examining lesson plans, rubrics, student work containing feedback, or exit tickets used to assess daily learning. For example, Susan asked Mary to share copies of rubrics she used in class. Susan wanted to see the rubric provided to students at the start of the assignment as well as examples of rubrics students had filled in as self-assessments and peer assessments. She also asked Mary for examples of the rubric with Mary's feedback and samples of student work. In this way, Susan could see the multiple uses for the rubric and could see how the students had improved their work following peer feedback. She noticed that Mary's students had used the rubric to guide their peer feedback, which resulted in peer assessments that supported the learning process and addressed the learning goals of the assignment.

Most likely, some combination of interviewing, direct observation, and document review will be needed for you to really see how your colleagues are using formative assessment practices to support student learning. You see that thread in what Susan did. Remember, Susan was interested in helping her students understand success criteria. She talked with Mary about the way Mary provided her students with success criteria. She arranged a time to observe Mary when she could see firsthand how Mary ensured that her students understood the success criteria on the assignment. And she came away from the class observation with examples of Mary's rubrics and Mary's students' work. Finally, Susan summarized what she learned in these discussions and observations and added the information to her *Self-Evaluation Record,* as shown in Figure 4.7.

| Figure 4.7 | Excerpt 4 From Susan's *Self-Evaluation Record* |

Teacher Self-Evaluation Record

Teacher Name: Susan B. **Content Area:** U.S. History

Step 2: Collecting Evidence of Practice (Continued)

Document Review Record	*Assignment rubric, student-filled rubrics, student work with rubric, and feedback*
Document Review Record	*I was really surprised at the level of detail she included in the rubric. I also noticed how it was really clear which learning expectations the assignment was aligned with.* *It also seemed like anyone could use this rubric to grade her student's projects. It was that specific. Student self- and peer evaluations were pretty accurate, and students were able to improve their work based on these evaluations. They had clear guidance for improving their work before it was due.*
What are the common practices/ideas I noticed from the interview, observation, and document review?	*Mary uses rubrics as a learning tool, not just a grading tool. These rubrics help students understand the learning expectations and evaluate their own work to make sure it is at the level of quality they want.*
What is the evidence that these practices work?	*On the last project, Mary's students on average scored 92 out of 100. This isn't because the assignment or the grading was easy. Her students just understood what she expected from them.*

Efforts to this point have focused on gathering information, evidence of sound formative evaluation practice, and its effects on student learning. The procedures we have described in previous paragraphs give you a large repository of ideas and examples that you can use to improve student learning in your classroom. When you collect a variety of types of evidence through interviews, observation, and document review, you are creating a set of resources for your own learning. This process parallels the learning process for your students when you engage them in formative assessment practices. You ask them to consult with their peers; observe you and their peers based on specific elements of a task; and examine documents, including lab notes, text readings, and rubrics.

With gathered materials in hand, take a little time to organize them for analysis purposes. Plan ahead, too, and arrange and locate them for long-term access as well. Things that are not well labeled and stored appropriately tend to be missing when you need them most.

Assessing Quality of Information

Assessment of collected information is largely a matter of review, analyzing obtained information to determine its fit with your objectives, culling information that is not relevant, and organizing the information in terms of your priority for use. If you have been following along with the steps presented in this chapter, you probably have collected information from a variety of sources to help you select a specific strategy or practice to try in your classroom. Is all the collected information equally helpful for your decision process, or do you view some aspects as more important? For example, you may notice that some of your colleagues use strategies that seem based on personal preference and would not be a good fit for you. Other colleagues may recommend assessment activities that you recognize as being summative rather than formative.

Mary organized information she had gathered and reviewed it to earmark higher priority material. In addition to interviewing and observing Mary, Susan had discussed assessment processes with colleagues in her professional learning community. Susan noted that some colleagues seemed to have different ideas about the practices that might be considered formative assessment. She reflected on whether their ideas would assist her in her efforts to implement formative assessment with her students.

Susan also reread the characteristics and examples in the *Formative Assessment Guide* to determine whether her colleagues' ideas were in line with the focus of formative assessment. Susan's colleague June described how she encouraged her students to use quarterly summaries of their grades to assess their own learning. Susan wondered whether June's students were really engaged in self-assessment through this strategy. After rereading Characteristic 4 and its examples, Susan determined that June's strategy seemed to be a way of helping students monitor their progress, but it didn't fit with the learning focus of formative assessment.

Not surprisingly, Susan retained and gave highest priority to the rubric ideas and material from Mary's class. This information best fit her intentions to improve in helping her students understand success criteria. Much of her analysis efforts then focused on how the rubric ideas fit into and could be complemented by suggestions from other colleagues.

Selecting an Area for Improvement

Choosing your focus for improvement should be a natural result of your evaluation efforts. Hopefully, your path toward that choice has gone something like the following. Using the *Self-Evaluation Record* to guide your review, you considered your own practices and discussed your practices with other teachers. Where relevant and feasible, you conducted a focused interview of a skilled colleague and perhaps observed that colleague during a lesson and looked at classroom artifacts that provided insight into aspects of formative assessment practice. All of these steps should have helped you refine your thinking and settle on a focus for improvement.

The next step is to choose a specific strategy to implement in your own classroom. When choosing a new strategy to implement, you might employ Goldilocks's selection criterion: not too big, not too small, but "just right." It's important to select a strategy that will fit with your teaching situation and will be unlikely to cause significant upheaval among your students; some upheaval, carefully explained and structured, is probably necessary. Most important, you want to select something with the potential to clearly improve student learning. Because this choice is so important, we designed the "Making a Plan to Implement a New Practice" section of the *Self-Evaluation Record* to help you with this step.

We designed the questions in the "Making a Plan" section of the *Self-Evaluation Record* to help you determine a practical, but meaningful, change that you can begin to implement. Part of the role of this section is to help you avoid gimmickry. It is important to remember that the goal of the change is to improve student learning rather than spice up the classroom!

Part of making a plan focuses on areas of practice that will have the greatest payoff for you and your students. Once those areas are determined, consider what is most practical and feasible for you. Figure 4.8 shows an example of two teachers' plans for beginning work on their practice.

Figure 4.8   Balancing Where to Start: Too Much Versus Too Little

Teacher A	Teacher B
• End each lesson with student self-report • Incorporate weekly feedback • Make learning goals for each lesson clear • Change grading practices	• Use rubrics to structure peer assessment once a semester

The teacher on the left, Teacher A, has selected an ambitious number of focus areas in her instruction. However, this is too much to start all at once. Her list will require significant changes to her routines, preparation, and student practices. Some areas, such as the use of peer feedback or the change to grading practices, are under-specified; therefore, she will need to do a great deal of additional planning to make her plan actionable. Although this enthusiasm and motivation is great, the teacher has likely bitten off too much to try to change all at once. She will eventually get there if she takes each idea and breaks it down into what specifically would be required. It is better to start out small with something clearly planned and achievable and build on that. Too many areas of focus, with not enough detail to implement, may mean nothing will get done.

By contrast, Teacher B on the right is being too cautious, having identified only one change to make in class on an infrequent basis. This change is not likely to produce any noticeable improvements in student learning and will fail to show how formative assessment can help improve student learning. This teacher should take on a slightly larger challenge.

Figure 4.9 The "Just Right" Starting Point

Teacher C: Before I can pay more attention to what my students understand during instruction, I first need to be sure that they know—and I know—the focus of the learning. For my third-period class each day, I will develop a clear statement of the learning goal for the lesson, focusing on the "learning," not the "doing." I will ask my team partner to meet with me once a week so that I can share the learning goals for the following week with her for feedback. To begin to have more formative assessment in my class, at the end of each lesson I will try to bring students back to the learning goal in a couple of ways:

1. With a specific targeted question that hones in on the major concept of that lesson. I can use this question to gather evidence to adjust my lesson plans or more generally poll the class to gauge their sense of their own understanding.

2. By explicitly reminding students of the learning goal so that they can tie ideas and concepts together.

Compare the Teacher A and B examples with the third example of a teacher planning how to change his practice in Figure 4.9. Teacher C has a single focus for his formative assessment development efforts. This focus will affect how he begins and ends his lessons.

While Teacher C's intention is to have a learning goal for each lesson, he is not necessarily going to try to have an aligned assessment question ready for the end of the lesson each day. On some days, he will settle for just making sure he reminds students at the end of the lesson what the learning goal was. He has bounded it by initially implementing his plan in only one class. In addition, he has identified one teacher that he can work with to test his learning goal statements. A plan like this lends itself to future expansion. As the process becomes more automatic, he can then expand it to his other classes, and he can try other ways of wrapping up the lesson to check on student learning progress.

Although he has a plan, he has left some leeway for implementing it. You, too, should plan with contingencies in mind. This flexibility can help you deal with unexpected classroom situations without feeling the need to give up on the whole process. With the addition of flexibility, the criteria we suggest for making a "just right" choice in formative assessment include single focus, well bounded (has limits), flexible implementation, and a clear path for expansion.

Compare Susan's choice of implementation plan with the four criteria. Susan decided to implement Mary's strategy of having students use assignment rubrics to evaluate student work. Her plan is shown in Figure 4.10.

"Just Right" Criteria

- Single focus
- Well bounded (has limits)
- Flexible implementation
- Clear path for expansion

Figure 4.10   Susan's "Just Right" Plan

At the beginning of the American Civil War unit, I will hand out the rubrics that I will use to assess the end-of-unit projects. I will also pass out three de-identified examples of projects from previous years: one that exceeded the project expectations, one that met the expectations, and one that did not meet the expectations. Without giving any description of the quality of the three projects, I will have students individually "grade" each of the examples using the rubric. Each example will then be discussed in class, and I will end by explaining to the students the scores that each paper received, and why. After seeing how this works, I plan to use it or a modification of the same idea with my other unit projects.

Susan's plan focuses solely on using rubrics to help establish a shared understanding of the success criteria. It is limited to one specific strategy that will take one class period. It is flexible in that Susan can redirect the conversation with students as needed or have students revisit the rubrics in the future. By starting with rubrics for just one project, she has a clear plan for expanding this strategy to future units.

Often, it is easier to implement a new strategy when starting a new topic or unit with your students. You will be able to organize the work for the unit around the strategy you have selected and maintain some consistency throughout the implementation. You also will be able to measure student progress more easily by concentrating on an identifiable portion of your curriculum. This means that the boundaries apply not just to your strategy, but also to your course material.

Susan used student grades on the American Civil War project as a measure of student progress. Since she had been giving the same assignment for several years, she was able to easily compare the performance of students from previous years with that of her current students who spent time reviewing project rubrics and examples of student work. (Web Tool C3 has the entire *Self-Evaluation Record* for Susan.)

As you work to implement your selected strategy, we encourage you to document the process, your experiences, and the student outcomes. You have to know what you did to repeat or change it to better make an impact on student learning. It also helps to know what parts were frustrating so you can deal better with them next time. We developed the questions in the "Self-Reflection After Implementing New Practice" section of the *Self-Evaluation Record* to assist you in the documentation. Alternatively, you may find that taking a few minutes at the end of the day or the lesson to "journal" to yourself provides sufficiently useful insights. Sharing your insights, successes, and frustrations with your learning community, a trusted colleague, or content coach also will support the change process you are undertaking. Chapters 5 and 6 will provide more detailed information on how to go about implementing and documenting changes to your teaching practices.

Act, Reflect, Revise

Your implementation of a formative assessment strategy is the "act" part of what we view as a three-step process: act, reflect, and revise. As you engage in this action, bear in mind that changes rarely go strictly as planned. One of our colleagues is fond of saying, "The only one who really wants change is a baby with a wet diaper—and sometimes even she complains!" Changing habitual ways of teaching is rarely easy or comfortable. Teachers typically develop habitual teaching strategies through a combination of learned behavior, comfort, and maybe even some past "experiments" (either explicit or implicit) and their results. Now we are asking you to explicitly define and conduct an "experiment" to improve your formative assessment practice—which we hope ultimately becomes a habitual practice.

In keeping with the goal of formative assessment practices, your actions are intended to improve student learning and your work as a teacher. At the outset, you may think that it is taking longer to do things than it has in the past since the routines are no longer routine. Bear in mind, however, that time is not the ultimate criterion. The end result should be to increase student engagement in learning and student ownership of their assessments.

When you implement formative assessment strategies, you also empower students to assess themselves and their peers in ways that lead to learning. The teacher's role shifts from being the only provider of constructive feedback to being one of a chorus of feedback providers—with a shared goal of success for all students. Expect that you will have to modify your actions in these regards to best serve student learning. We attend directly to such revisions in Chapter 5, where we focus on the reflect and revise aspects of the act-reflect-revise process.

Summary: The Big Idea of Chapter 4

Having selected a broad area of practice to consider changing (Chapter 3), the next stage is to engage in a more detailed investigation of that characteristic. This investigation includes a variety of facets and actions: self-reflection, data collection about exemplary practice related to that characteristic, interviews with colleagues, classroom observation, and document review. Likely your own planning efforts will include several, if not all, of those actions. Here we introduced two tools to assist your investigation. The *Formative Assessment Guide* assists your determination of a focus and helps you consider major facets of your point of focus. The *Self-Evaluation Record* provides support and guidance as you move through this process. The fruits of these actions will at this point yield a plan for your use in trying some new strategies in your classroom.

Questions for Individual Consideration

1) As you think about the characteristics of formative assessment, or one of its components, what evidence sources do you think will be most useful as you examine this area in more depth?

2) What resources can you draw on for this self-evaluation?

Questions for Consideration as a Learning Community

1) Are there any parts of the process described in this chapter that are unclear? If so, can someone in the group clarify them for you?

2) Think about each characteristic of formative assessment. Of the various ways in which you can collect evidence of practice—interviews, observations, document review—which one(s) seems more appropriate for each characteristic or component?

5

Support for Making Changes to Practice

As we discussed at several points in this book, the overall process of improving your formative assessment practices is a cyclical one (Figure 5.1). Within Step 3 of that overall process is another cycle for improving the particular practice you have chosen to work on: act, reflect, and revise. In this cycle within a cycle, highlighted in the gray box in Figure 5.1, you will try out some new practices in your classroom, reflect on them, and revise as necessary. Our goal is to help you successfully implement the formative assessment changes you have planned. We begin by discussing how that cycle relates to the work you have done in previous chapters and walk you through the cycle for implementing the practices you have chosen. Because implementation can be a challenging step in the process, we have included examples to show how you can find help—actions that you can take and people who can support you.

To recap, after the examples and overview of formative assessment in Chapter 2, we stepped through a process in Chapter 3 for thinking about your formative assessment practice to select an area on which to focus. We suggested three approaches for you to use: (a) the *Formative Assessment Practices Survey*; (b) discussion with your colleagues; and (c) reflection on your current practice by using the definitions and characteristics of formative assessment and considering

Figure 5.1 The Cycle-Within-the-Cycle Process: Implementing Change

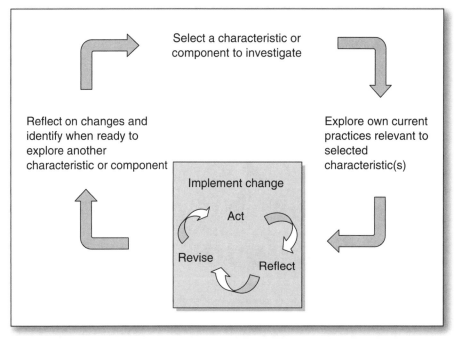

both your students' previous experiences with formative assessment and your specific teaching context. In Chapter 4 we shared a process for a more in-depth investigation of your selected area of focus by using two tools: the *Formative Assessment Guide* and the *Self-Evaluation Record.* The tools are intended to guide and support the process as you collect additional information through interviews with colleagues, classroom observations, and/or document review.

We ended Chapter 4 by asking you to make a specific plan of action for the formative assessment changes you want to try out in your classroom. In Chapter 5 we focus on implementing those changes. Our goal through the use of the act-reflect-revise cycle is in part to remind you that change is an ongoing process.

The Cycle Within the Cycle: Act, Reflect, Revise

In this section, we discuss the act-reflect-revise cycle (adapted from Thompson & Wiliam, 2008). Using this cycle within the cycle, we show you how to try out new formative assessment practices as you continue with your regular instruction. You will implement the plan you created using the "just right" criteria in Chapter 4, which we hope will be possible to enact within your current schedule.

The first part of the act-reflect-revise cycle addresses action. It is not enough to have a plan for change: you must implement the plan. One school of thought is that you have to do something for 21 days to form a habit. Recent research suggests that it can take an average of 66 days to form a new habit (Lally, van Jaarsveld, Potts, & Wardle, 2010). On one hand, 66 days sounds daunting. On the other hand, consider how many times a teacher could repeat certain actions over 10 years in the classroom. Something that might be done once per lesson could add up to six times per day and 1,080 times per year, which is almost 11,000 repetitions in a decade of teaching. What the real number of trials to reach habit status requires likely is neither 21 days nor 66 days. The point is that even when you and your students are highly motivated to develop new habits, building a habit requires time and perseverance.

You might easily incorporate some changes into your practice if they are simple. For example, asking students for a show of thumbs up or thumbs down to indicate their level of understanding of a new concept can be applied quickly. Even that action, though, takes practice for it to become a habit. Other changes take more repetitions to get them right.

Some changes might seem straightforward initially, but the actual enactment of the idea requires significantly more thinking and planning than you initially thought. Presenting learning expectations in a lesson is one example. You might not find it difficult to remember to write a learning expectation on the board at the start of each lesson, but you may find it challenging to craft a quality learning expectation for every lesson when you are planning.

For some lessons, you might struggle to articulate what it is exactly that you want students to learn. *To Kill a Mockingbird* is considered a classic text, but what is it that you want students to learn from it? If your next science unit is going to focus on density, what do students need to learn lesson by lesson? The Civil War is an important period in American history, but what do you want students to have learned at the end of the unit?

Given the challenges you might face, planning for repetition of your new assessment practices allows you the space to acknowledge that your first efforts will not be perfect. Some days you will not express the learning expectation in the best language or get at the heart of what you really intended students to learn. However, once you have begun implementing your plan, you are then able to move through the other two steps in the cycle: reflect and revise.

Through the reflect-and-revise steps, you can improve your formative assessment practice over time. Reflection on your formative assessment practice means to step back from what you attempted to change to consider what was successful and where you struggled. The revision step is also essential. It means that just because something was not as successful as you would have liked, you do not just abandon the practice. As you reflect on what happened, you may be able to come up with an alternative approach or an adjustment that might help. Even a successful attempt has room for improvement.

Some changes to practice may disrupt the routines or norms you have established in your classroom. You may be asking your students to take on new roles or think about their learning in different ways. Those changes all take practice for them as well as you; thus, the reflection and revision steps give you room to make adjustments.

Part of what we emphasize is the use of structures to support your reflection on practice. Some of these structures will be useful whether you work alone or with others. In the following section on learning communities, we talk more about structures that you can use with peers to support reflection. Chapter 6 provides additional resources to support your engaging in a more formal type of reflection—or evaluation—of the changes you make to your formative assessment practices.

The final section of the *Self-Evaluation Record* is called "Self-Reflection After Implementing a New Practice." This section has a series of prompts that you may find useful to structure your reflection. How did things go when I implemented the new practices? What about my self-reflection after implementing the new practices? What evidence supports my self-reflection? This section of the form is an appropriate place to record some changes that you might want to make in future uses of the formative assessment practice.

The earlier example of writing learning expectations illustrates where reflection and revision come into play. After you teach a lesson, for example, you can reflect on whether your statement of the learning expectation accurately encompassed the lesson. You can consider what evidence you have that students understood or did not understand what you did or why and whether it seemed to be effective in achieving what you intended. Sometimes you can identify that a particular action you took did not go well, but struggle to put your finger on the specific issue. In those cases, you might need a sounding board; talking it over with a peer or coach may help. Once you identify specific reasons why an action was not as successful as you would like, you can revise it. Again, you may need to draw on a teaching partner, coach, or other resources beyond your own thinking.

The timing of your revisions also may vary. In the context of the learning expectations, you may adjust immediately and present the learning expectations differently to the students in the next lesson, or you may make a note in your lesson planning for the following year. In the box, we present an example of a teacher who was making some changes to her formative assessment practice and how she used both reflection and revision to deal with some setbacks.

Tracy was a mathematics teacher who had recently transitioned to sixth grade, having previously taught elementary students. She initially had focused on finding ways to increase the amount of feedback that she provided to students. Next, she worked on using the information she gathered about student learning to make adjustments to her instructional plans. As these new skills became a part of her everyday practice, she decided to explore self-assessment in her classroom, because she realized that she had never given students the opportunity to develop this skill. She knew that students would need some coaching to become good self-assessors. She decided that although this area sounded very challenging, her students could truly benefit from assessing themselves as a way to self-monitor and become more vested in their own learning.

Tracy found student self-assessments in her curriculum resources and photo-copied one for each student. She had them complete the self-assessment form about a week prior to a planned unit test on identifying properties of angles and triangles. When she got the student responses back, she was surprised and disappointed by what they wrote. Most of the students had difficulty answering the questions and many had put "IDK" (I don't know) on the majority of the questions.

She met with her coach to discuss what had happened. In reviewing the self-assessment questions with the coach, Tracy realized that her students had never been asked to think deeply about their learning or learning topics. She had assumed that posting her learning expectations on the board and telling them to students along with reviewing skills checklists, rubrics, and exemplars at the outset of learning was sufficient to prepare the students to be good self-assessors.

In light of their responses to her first self-assessment, she made a plan to scaffold students' learning. First, she modeled for students what self-assessment might look like in class by working a problem "thinking aloud" to the students, purposefully making some small errors and then completing a self-assessment of her ability to successfully solve the problem. Then she asked each student to fill out a skills checklist, describing his or her level of perceived skill development during that unit. Finally, Tracy presented them with the end-of-unit self-evaluation questions, again modeling possible answers to each question first. This time, her students had a little more success. She continued this practice at the end of each unit, reducing the amount of modeling as they became more familiar with the process. Over time, students became more reflective on their learning outcomes, and they were better able to target their learning in the final week before a unit test.

We can apply the act-reflect-revise cycle to Tracy's experience. First, she identified the area of student self-assessment as the place where she wanted to try out some changes. She was able to find some resources to use to support her action. She was surprised (and disappointed) by the initial responses from her students and used her coach as a sounding board to talk through the experience. Through this conversation, she was able to develop a revised plan of action to more slowly scaffold the experience for students and to remove the supports gradually over time. She examined how well the revised plan worked by continuing to collect information from the students, who showed greater proficiency over time.

It is important to remember that most implementations of changes to practice will need some revision. To make appropriate adjustments, it is also important to take the time to reflect on how the initial action really went. Although Tracy could have been disheartened because the results of her initial "act" showed that students did not know what they needed to do, Tracy took those results as a challenge to think more about what was going on and to use her coach to help her figure that out. Her example also illustrates the importance of having support structures in place. The remainder of the chapter addresses a number of different supports and provides several examples of how teachers used those supports.

Sources of Support

While you can implement and use the act-reflect-revise cycle on your own, it is likely to be more effective if you have colleagues you can talk with to share ideas, give and receive feedback, and discuss each other's formative assessment approaches. In this section, we review three sources of support for you as you engage in improving your formative assessment practice: peers in a learning community, coaches and mentors, and supervisors and administrators. The nature of the support may vary according to their role, but each can provide important help.

For each source of support, we describe what it is, provide some research basis for why we consider it to be worthwhile, examine how the approach provides support, and offer some additional considerations for how to get the maximum benefit from each one. In addition, we include three examples of how these sources of support have played out for teachers. Because the examples are long, we have kept them to the very end of the chapter.

Learning Communities

In Chapter 1, we mentioned that you might use this book either on your own or as part of a learning community. You have seen that we have included questions at the end of each chapter that might be useful in the context of a learning community. Thus, it should not come as any surprise when we say that a group of your peers is an important source of support for you in developing and improving your formative assessment practice.

A learning community is a group of teachers who meet on a regular basis to learn together and from each other (DuFour, 2004). A learning community may cross multiple grade levels or be composed of teachers who all teach the same grade or content area. In part, the composition depends on the nature of the learning focus and can vary over time. You may be able to engage with formalized professional learning communities already in place in your school, or you may form a group on your own with some of your colleagues.

As you consider creating or simply participating in a learning community, we encourage you to consider and discuss recent research findings. This can help you figure out how to structure one in your school. For example, the National Staff Development Council's report on professional learning (Darling-Hammond, Wei, Andree, Richardson, & Orphanos, 2009) examined experimental studies on professional development. Their report makes four recommendations about professional development. First, it should be intensive, ongoing, and connected to practice. Second, professional development should focus on student learning and address the teaching of specific curriculum content. Third, professional development should align with school improvement priorities and goals. Finally, professional development should build strong working relationships among teachers. As Wylie and Lyon (2009) described, professional learning communities can meet all four of these recommendations, when they are established for the purpose of supporting teachers in improving their professional practice.

A learning community can serve multiple purposes. It provides a forum for learning about new formative assessment ideas. It gives members opportunities to talk about the application of new ideas to practice to get feedback. And the community provides a structure for members to learn from each other's experience. As with most things, a learning community's usefulness is determined in part by the care taken in setting it up and managing its practices.

We suggest that you consider three facets of learning communities as you embark in their use. First, provide a forum for learning about formative assessment by using a common set of materials. Members of the learning community can select materials to read and review about formative assessment or look for online resources that might provide videos of other teachers engaged in formative assessment. These resources set the stage for discussion and improvement. For example, critiquing the videos and discussing how they might apply to your own practice can be a powerful source of learning. Using such materials is a good starting point for learning communities because they focus on people and situations outside your own learning community. Discussion of such materials can be helpful with less risk of being divisive.

Second, the learning community is a place where you have opportunities to discuss applications of new ideas to your practice and get feedback. It is only when learning is applied to practice that change can take place. The learning community allows you to reflect on what worked and what was not yet successful; it provides you with a group of colleagues who can ask questions to help you think more deeply about your practice or provide suggestions to help you move forward. From this support, you may make modifications to your practice—in other words, reflect and revise.

Third, the learning community benefits other individuals in the group as well as the group as a whole. Just as you learn from others when your practice is going well, the other members can benefit from lessons you have learned. Someone else in the group may be trying something similar to your actions, but in a less successful way, and can learn from you. Your success in one particular area also may motivate someone else to try it out in their classroom.

Groupwide benefits go beyond individual gains. Learning communities can develop a positive spirit. Certainly, the spirit grows from individual willingness to experiment and share. Yet, that community spirit has a way of encouraging all in the group. That spirit can keep you going when things do not go as you had hoped. Generally, like a rising tide lifts all boats, all the experiences that group members can draw upon help everyone do better as a result.

Benefits of a Learning Community

1. It provides a forum to learn about new formative assessment ideas.

2. It provides a group of people with whom you can discuss new ideas and get feedback.

3. The collective learning of the group benefits everyone.

As a group, learning communities also can improve accountability. We believe it is important to find ways to have members hold each other accountable. At the same time, you must ensure that members within the learning community get support and feedback.

Creating a set of group norms or expectations can serve the learning community's effectiveness and accountability. Norms and expectations help keep the learning community focused and on task—maintaining focus is often the most challenging aspect of learning communities. These norms and expectations come in a variety of forms. Some relate to group behavior and meeting focus that can help keep discussions on target. Others are best described as group routines, activities done on a regular basis, or activities that no one can shirk.

Weight Watchers® is not about formative assessment, but it does provide a nice example of how routines can be helpful. Weight Watchers, a successful weight loss approach, employs a group context of accountability in the form of regular weigh-ins. Even if someone has cheated with his or her diet for a couple of days, knowing that weigh-in day is coming can motivate the individual to get back on track.

The Weight Watchers example illustrates how routines can provide a helpful structure for meetings: weigh-in, followed by a discussion of progress, followed by a discussion on a related topic of interest. Similarly, when teachers meet in a learning community, it is important to have a routine or set of routines that can be drawn on so that formative assessment remains the central focus. Otherwise, it can be easy to drift into discussing other topics like student behavior or the impact of a new district mandate.

Just as Weight-Watchers-type routines help ensure preparation and meeting focus, so, too, should your meeting routines ensure sharing of formative assessment practice information. As noted early in this chapter, a major value of the learning community comes from sharing your practice with others. This sharing supports your reflection on practice and enables you to get advice or feedback on how you might revise an existing practice.

One potential downside of sharing within learning communities is that discussions can drift off task. A variety of factors can cause this drift. For example, someone may have a funny story, there may be a major coming event, or someone may be stressed out on matters outside the school. The cause of drift may be as simple as the number of people in your community, because more people mean more distractions. Distractions can detract from your community's structure and discourage accountability. For that reason, we conclude this section with four actions to structure the sharing of formative assessment practice within your learning community.

First, we encourage you to establish a set of guidelines, or expectations, for discussion focus. For example, prompts such as Who? When? What? How? and Why? can provide a structure to ensure that you talk about who was involved (both your role and your students' roles); when or for how long; what specifically was done; how it was done; and, most important, why it was done. If you provide incomplete information, your colleagues in the learning community can ask additional questions, such as "I understand what you did, but can you say some more about why?" This structure supports both the person sharing and the listeners.

Second, you can help keep focus while sharing practice by checking whether you can relate your description of practice to one of the four characteristics of formative assessment. If you cannot easily connect the practice to the four characteristics, it raises the question of whether this practice is centered on formative assessment. In some cases, you might be able to make some changes and return it to its formative nature. In others, you might realize that you had focused on something more closely related to behavior management or another aspect of teaching. That focus, while important, is not the focus of the formative-assessment-focused professional learning community. Your group may need to develop signals or procedures to bring a drifting discussion back on topic. One group of teachers in the Midwest created badges that said, "What's formative about that?" and would use that question to redirect conversation.

A third way you can structure a discussion among a group of teachers and promote reflection is to share the classroom product that went along with the practice. Rather than talk generally about your use of exit tickets or the kind of feedback you give students, bring those materials to the learning community. Share the specific exit ticket you used, examples of feedback you wrote on student papers, or the learning expectation you posted on the board.

Sharing concrete examples in your learning communities allows you and your peers to learn more effectively from one another. By allowing your peers to see exactly what you did, you enable them to provide more specific feedback than if you just gave a general description of the process—and specific feedback is ultimately more useful than general feedback. For example, your approach to using the exit ticket question might sound exemplary; but when your peers see the actual question on the exit ticket, it allows them to consider whether it addressed the learning expectation. Similarly, your description of writing feedback to students might sound too time-consuming to some teachers. Showing them the specifics of what you wrote and what students did with that feedback can make a powerful argument for the value of formative feedback.

Fourth, provide structure to ensure presentations of progress at your meetings and for individual presentations as well. Both kinds of structure serve learning community effectiveness. Providing a structure for individual presentations makes it easier for individuals to prepare to present. This structure also provides a way for listeners to parse what they are hearing.

When you structure group meetings in a way that calls for sharing-of-progress presentations, you raise the importance of progress reports and enhance group accountability. That structure ensures that progress reports will always be part of the meeting. Accountability is enhanced because expectations for sharing also encourage preparation by some who would otherwise come unprepared. The idea of group accountability is the reason that many runners join running clubs. Knowing that a group is waiting for you can motivate you to run on a rainy day whereas, left to your own devices, you might decide not to run. Similarly, when midyear report cards and parent-teacher conferences can be all-consuming, it might be tempting to not introduce a new formative assessment practice to your class. But knowing that the group will be expecting it and interested to hear how it went at your next meeting might be sufficient encouragement for you to give it a go.

Structures to Help a Learning Community Function

1. Offer structures to support sharing of practice (e.g., Who? When? What? How? Why?).

2. Ensure everyone connects practice back to the four characteristics of formative assessment.

3. Share the classroom product that goes along with the practice (e.g., the specific feedback you wrote on some student work).

4. Provide group norms for routines and behaviors.

You will see some of these structural characteristics in the Jason case example near the end of this chapter. Jason was assisted by a learning community as he worked to improve his formative assessment practice. In that example, the learning community provided feedback to help Jason identify an area to work on. They also provided concrete examples of how they operationalized this aspect of formative assessment. Once Jason began to implement new ideas in his classroom, the group continued to act as a resource for him. In addition, it continued to meet regularly so they could learn together from one another's experiences.

Coaches or Mentors

Like a learning community, coaches or mentors can effectively support formative assessment development efforts. Their role, however, differs from that provided by a learning community and can provide several advantages over a learning community. The assumption in a learning community is that everyone is learning together and that everyone is trying to incorporate more formative assessment practice into their instruction. Consider the earlier example of working on learning expectations. If your struggle is specifically with framing the learning expectation for lessons in a particular unit, you would need, and the learning community many not be able to provide, someone with more content knowledge or teaching experience to work with you. This is a role that a coach or mentor can serve well. (Throughout this section, we use the term *coach,* which is often defined as an instructional expert who guides teachers, but we recognize that this support role also could be played less formally with a mentor.)

The use of instructional coaches has become increasingly common, especially in the context of distributed leadership in schools. However, there is a smaller research base to support their effectiveness. A primer by Knight (2005) identified some critical characteristics: coaches need to be highly qualified, focus on appropriate teaching methods, and partner with teachers. Over time, these meaningful collaborations support the development of excellent teachers.

A coach or supervisor likely has two advantages over an equally qualified classroom teacher. One advantage is that he or she is not tied to a rigid teaching schedule. So while a colleague who teaches classes similar to yours may not be able to join you in your classroom, a coach or a supervisor may be able to do that. A second advantage that a coaching model can offer is that coaches can focus specifically on your needs and context.

Benefits of a Coach or Mentor

1. Greater flexibility in terms of a coach's schedule to come to your classroom

2. Support targeted to your specific needs and context

Several reasons and occasions may call for involvement by a coach. You may be asking for coteaching support, for feedback on a specific aspect of your formative assessment practice, or for the coach to implement an approach that you are interested in, but unsure about. Whatever the reason, it is important to ensure that both of you are clear about the purpose of the visit.

Four occasions that may prompt you to invite a coach to your classroom include (a) when you want support to try an unfamiliar formative assessment strategy with your students, (b) when you want feedback on a new approach that you have been implementing, (c) when you would like to observe a demonstration lesson to help you better understand how to implement a new approach, or (d) when you want to observe another teacher and need someone to take over your class. Each of these four occasions has a different purpose, roles for you and the coach, and required preparation. We conclude this section with a set of examples that illustrate these four coaching roles.

The first occasion in which a coach can play a role is to provide support for the implementation of a new strategy, both in terms of planning and actual implementation. Imagine you were interested in having students work together in small groups, using a rubric, to give feedback to their peers on a project. If working in small groups is an unfamiliar strategy for your class, you might want to work with a coach or mentor to develop a plan for how to organize the class. Certainly, it can also be advantageous to have an extra pair of hands in the classroom while students adjust to new roles. In this instance, the coach may take on a coteaching role. You would prepare for engaging the coach much as you would prepare to include another teacher in your classroom.

A second occasion in which a coach can play a role is to provide feedback when you have tried out something new and want a different perspective on which to reflect. In this instance, the coach is taking on the role of a classroom observer. The planning and setup for this kind of visit will be a little different compared with the previous coteaching role.

To prepare, you would want to provide some context to the coach about what you had been trying and the specific nature of the feedback you would like. For example, say you are focused on opening and closing the class period with the learning expectations. Too often, you have found this process challenging because the bell for the end of the class period has rung before you have had an opportunity to regroup with your students.

You might invite the coach to observe the starts and ends of several lessons during an entire school day in order to give you some advice on time management strategies. You may not always have as specific a request for the coach as this learning intention example, but you probably want to narrow the scope of the observation for it to be most beneficial. This kind of observation is not intended to be part of any formal observation in which you are required to participate for your school or personnel evaluation process. It should be purely for the purpose of helping you reflect on a new practice.

The third occasion in which a coach, mentor, or supervisor can play a role is when you want to observe a demonstration lesson that models a specific formative assessment approach. You might be interested in trying something new, but realize that just hearing a description of how it should go from a colleague may not be enough. Seeing is sometimes better.

Again, the roles and preparation in this context are different. In advance of the lesson, both you and the coach need to be clear about specific lesson goals, about the formative assessment strategy you want to observe, and that it is appropriate for the content to be taught. Another aspect of preparation would be to consider what your role will be so that you get the most benefit from the lesson. Do you want to observe from the front or back of the classroom? Do you want to sit with a group of students? What do you need to tell students in advance of the lesson? In this instance, the coach is taking on the role of the instructor, while your role is that of an observer.

The final occasion in which a coach can play a role is when you would like to work with a colleague. The coach can support your growth and development by freeing up a colleague who teaches in your subject area to come to your classroom (or allowing you to go to the other teacher's classroom) in order to coteach, observe, or conduct a demonstration lesson. In other words, the coach could take over the classroom of your peer for a lesson period while he or she comes to your classroom. This may be a useful approach if, for example, the coach is not as familiar with your curriculum material—or the formative assessment approaches—as your colleague might be. Obviously, this takes additional planning since two classrooms now are having some disruptions.

Reasons to Invite a Coach to Your Classroom

1. When you want support to try an unfamiliar formative assessment strategy with your students

2. When you want feedback on a new approach that you have been implementing

3. When you would like to observe a demonstration lesson to help you better understand how to implement a new approach

4. When you want to observe another teacher and need someone to take over your class

Regardless of your coach's role, it is important that you and the coach debrief the experience together. This is especially important when your coach has served as a coteacher, provider of feedback, or demonstrator in your classroom. What did you learn from the experience? What can you now apply to your own instruction? What future support do you need?

One of the case examples at the close of this chapter includes a description of how a coach helped a teacher improve her formative assessment practice. In that example, the coach served as a sounding board as Carol worked through the initial steps of the self-evaluation process. Once Carol had selected an area of focus, her coach modeled a specific technique in a lesson, and provided ongoing feedback based on classroom observations.

Administrators or Supervisors

This section focuses on school administrators or supervisors as a third source of support that you can call on to help you implement the act-reflect-revise cycle. The support role played by peers who are trying out formative assessment ideas in their classrooms along with you will be quite different from the support that you might get from a coach or mentor. In turn, that support may be quite different from the kinds of support you can get from your principal or other school administrators. So what kind of support can your school principal provide? The support varies substantially depending on the expertise and experience of the respective principal.

Several studies speak to the important impacts principals have in their schools. Boyd et al. (2011) found relationships between principals' characteristics and teacher retention that have a positive effect on school climate. Similarly, Quinn (2002) found positive effects related to instructional practice and student engagement. More generally, findings by Hallinger and Heck (1998) and by Marzano, Waters, and McNulty (2005) indicated that principals contribute to school effectiveness, which suggests that it is important to engage their support as you explore how to improve your formative assessment practice.

Some principals are able to engage in substantive discussions about teaching and learning issues, but not all can. Certainly, not all can be experts in the subject area you teach. The principal who has previously taught the same content area or grade level as you teach may be able to offer the same support a coach does.

Your school principal may not have taught the same grade level or content area as you. If that is the case, your principal might support your formative assessment efforts in less direct, but equally important, ways as coaching. The principal might supervise another teacher's class so that she can visit your class to observe, coteach, or work with you to prepare formative assessment materials (e.g., learning expectations for the next week or two). Just the principal's willingness to visibly demonstrate that teacher learning is important and valued is a critical role.

Principals often have considerable say in or direct control over the scheduling and logistics of the school. One of the most practical ways a principal can support teachers who wish to improve their formative assessment practice is to ensure that they have time to meet, either as a formal learning community or in some other way. This can require creative scheduling or working with a variety of stakeholders to ensure that schedule changes are handled sensitively. What works in one context may not work in another.

Support You Can Get From Administrators or Supervisors

1. As an instructional leader to discuss issues surrounding formative assessment

2. As an additional resource to supervise a teacher's classroom

3. As a leader who can engage in creative scheduling and coordination to find time for teachers to meet in learning communities

---

At the end of this chapter, we have included a description about an administrator. In this example, an elementary principal was able to work creatively with the school schedule to ensure that all teachers were able to participate in school-based learning communities on a weekly basis. His actions made it possible for grade-level teachers to work together on their formative assessment practice.

How Will I Know When I Am Ready to Choose a New Target or Characteristic?

We recommend that you do not try to change too many things in your practice (think back to the not-too-small-not-too-large example of the previous chapter). However, once a new formative assessment practice has become habitual for both you and your students, it will no longer require as much attention. For instance, if your students now expect to start a lesson with a learning expectation and you have developed routines with a teaching partner for writing some expectations for each week, perhaps you are ready to look again at your *Formative Assessment Practices Survey* and *Self-Evaluation Record* to select another area of focus.

To develop a well-rounded formative assessment practice, you need to attend to all four characteristics, not just stick with one that has become comfortable. Another way to think of this is in terms of a computer analogy—when you have enough processing space in your mind for extra activity, it may be time to take a next step or include other attributes.

Another reason it might be time to try a new approach is if you are continuing to struggle with the implementation. Perhaps you or your students are lacking prerequisite skills, or the way you have chosen to change your practice does not fit your preferred teaching style. You may need to spend a little time reflecting to determine the cause of your struggle, just so that you do not dismiss a potentially valuable strategy. It may be that you consider the approach doable, but the payoffs are not sufficient to warrant the time and energy that is required in the setup. Another reason to take on a new skill or approach for your formative assessment practice is to acknowledge the growth you are experiencing. As you become more familiar with formative assessment, you can begin to see how the four characteristics are interwoven. You will begin to see practices not as distinct tasks you or your students do, but one as integral to another. For instance, giving meaningful feedback to students is made easier when both you and the students have a clear understanding of the learning expectations. Modeling good feedback for students supports them as they begin to give feedback to their peers. Taking on additional challenges in your own practice allows you to make those connections more easily and ultimately will make your impact on student learning greater.

Whatever your reason for venturing forth to try a new formative assessment approach, we think you will find the following case examples helpful to you. These examples describe the efforts of two teachers and a principal. Both teachers engage in new formative assessment practice, and each has a different support structure to serve that work. Jason worked within a learning community, and Carol worked with a coach. James was a school principal seeking to support teacher working groups. These support structures, of course, affect the ways in which teachers learn and apply formative assessment. They also change the options and opportunities to evaluate formative assessment practices to determine their effects. In Chapter 6, we address in more depth the issue of evaluating your progress to address the question, "Was the change worth it?" The process of collecting evidence of the impact of changes to your practices on students will provide a great deal of information that may contribute to the kind of reflection and revision we have talked about in this chapter.

Jason: Implementing Change With the Help of a Learning Community

Jason was a beginning eighth-grade science teacher at a Title I (high poverty) middle school. After he completed the *Formative Assessment Practices Survey*, Kelli, an instructional coach, suggested that he partner with some other science teachers in the building, who had more experience with formative assessment, to form a learning community. Jason's formative assessment learning community began to meet once a week after staff and department meetings.

At their first meeting, all the members shared the results of their *Formative Assessment Practices Survey* and read through the *Formative Assessment Guide*. Then they discussed their personal strengths and targeted areas for development. This discussion helped Jason realize two things: he was already doing some things well, and even the most experienced teachers had areas for improvement. The group spent time focused on each member to help clarify that teacher's thinking around an area they thought they wanted to work on. Jason chose to talk about the issue of his eighth-grade students' performance on the unit tests in spite of the fact that he had covered all the lessons. From the discussion, he was reminded that just because he had taught the lessons did not necessarily mean that students had learned them.

Other, more experienced, members of the learning community thought that Jason was always surprised by the test results of his students because he was not monitoring student progress regularly and checking for understanding prior to the unit test. They suggested Jason could add some simple formative assessments. These assessments could help him find out if students were ready for the test or if they needed alternative experiences or different explanations of the content, and so forth. They suggested that Jason focus his efforts on Characteristic 2. Specifically, the group thought he needed to work on the second and third components, which involve using formative assessment throughout learning experiences and checking for student understanding.

Based on the group's discussion and recommendation, Jason decided that he wanted to add some formative assessments to his lessons. However, he had some difficulty understanding exactly what these formative assessments might look like. The learning community decided to bring and discuss examples of formative assessments at their next meeting. Serena, another science teacher in the group, invited Jason to observe her classes.

During Jason's observation of Serena's class, he noticed her walking around the room with a clipboard, occasionally marking things down on it after she interacted with students. She later explained to him that another teacher in the learning community had helped her figure out how to keep track of student progress on a daily basis by using a checklist. The checklist included the name of each student from a class listed down the side and the learning goals of the unit listed at the top, one per column. She showed Jason how he could use the checklist to keep track of student progress. It seemed to him that this would add a lot of work to his already full plate of grading for 120 students. She explained that the information was not to be piled in a corner of her desk for grading later. The purpose of the checklist was to keep track of student learning *that day* so she would know how to accommodate for student differences in learning the next day. The clipboard checklist made it easy for her to track how well students responded to questions during class and which students she had not heard from, and whether she needed to adjust her instruction for the next day.

At one learning community meeting, another teacher, Mark discussed the concept of exit tickets and brought along a few examples. He explained that he used the exit tickets a few times a week and would have students respond to open-ended questions pertaining to the lesson that was delivered that day. These student responses gave him clues as to what students had achieved toward the daily learning objective. Jason really liked this idea because it was a simple, well-designed question that would really force him to think about the critical learning for a lesson that he wanted to assess. In addition, he would be able to review short student responses practically as the next class was gathering. He also thought that these exit tickets helped refocus the class on the learning objective.

Jason decided to implement exit tickets in his eighth-grade science class two or three times a week. While assigning the exit ticket, Jason used the time to summarize and have students share what they had learned. After completing their exit tickets, students left the room, handing their slips to Jason on the way out.

As Jason began to collect data using these formative assessment techniques, he realized that his learning community had been correct. Many times, when he thought students had really learned the material well, in actuality, the formative assessment activity showed they had misconceptions or really did not understand the content as well as he thought they had. Jason used this information to make immediate corrections to his teaching rather than just moving on with new material. For some concepts, he also went back to members of the learning community for ideas about alternative ways to present the concept. He shared some of the exit ticket questions he produced with another eighth-grade teacher so that together they could develop a resource for both of them to use.

Over time, Jason noticed that student performance on the unit tests began to get better. He thought it was because students had multiple opportunities to learn the material, whereas before, students had one shot at the material and then he had moved on to the next topic in the curriculum guide. In addition, Jason noticed that as his students became more proficient with the science content, they also began to enjoy science class more and became more eager and active participants in each day's activities.

Adding frequent formative assessments throughout the learning of a unit began to be part of Jason's normal routine. He continued to discuss his progress and concerns with his learning community, but no longer felt overwhelmed by the formative assessment improvement process.

Carol: Support Roles Provided by a Coach

Carol taught seventh- and eighth-grade mathematics and had previously worked with Anne, an instructional coach. Carol expressed an interest in thinking more about formative assessment, but admitted she was unsure where to start. Carol and Anne worked through the *Formative Assessment Practices Survey* and used Carol's responses to focus on Characteristic 2, "Formative assessment opportunities are designed to collect quality evidence to inform teaching and improve learning," as the focus for her self-evaluation and planning.

Working with Anne, Carol downloaded the *Self-Evaluation Record* to help guide her through the process and document her self-evaluation. Carol first considered recent lessons she had taught and asked for Anne's feedback about strategies she was already using to collect evidence about student learning. Through conversations with Anne, Carol realized that she relied too heavily on student performance on daily homework coupled with tests for most of her information about student learning. Those two sources limited the analysis that she could do of her instruction. Anne reminded Carol that her students also practiced new skills by completing problems at the board before starting their homework, although she did not necessarily get information from every student using this approach. However, Anne noted several instances in which Carol had retaught specific parts of a lesson based on the student mistakes she saw in their at-the-board practicing.

Carol then moved to the "Collecting evidence of practice" section of the *Self-Evaluation Record*. Given that Carol was focused on issues of feasibility with respect to increased use of formative assessment during instruction, she asked Anne to recommend colleagues who were using formative assessment to inform their teaching and who seemed to have found efficiencies with what they were doing. Because they did not share a planning period, Anne offered to set up an after-school meeting with two colleagues to start the discussions.

Carol met briefly with the recommended colleagues and learned about two formative assessment practices they used to collect evidence of student learning. First, they discussed "30-second share." The teacher set aside three to four minutes at the end of a lesson for students to paraphrase the key ideas. One student would start by saying one thing he or she had learned and would call on a second student to add to this, who then called on another one. It moved quickly and gave the teacher a different perspective on student learning. Second, they talked about guided practice activities in which all students were asked to solve a problem on whiteboards, using the skills presented during the lesson. The students held up the whiteboards with their answers for the teacher to see. Carol wondered how her colleagues assessed student performance beyond whether they came up with the correct answer on the whiteboards. She learned that her colleagues typically asked the students to determine which answer was correct and to explain how they made their determinations. In this way, the students demonstrated the thought processes that led them to their answers.

Carol and Anne met during Carol's planning period and discussed some monitoring devices that Carol wanted to try. Anne visited the class to model the use of whiteboards to monitor individual progress. Carol decided to incorporate the whiteboard activity to replace the at-the-board problem solving her students had been doing in class so that she would have information about all students, not just the few she selected to go to the board. After a few weeks, Anne noticed that Carol was using this strategy less often and had returned to the at-the-board activity. Carol told Anne that she had found that it was time-consuming for her to use the whiteboards because there were too many variations in how her students arrived at their answers. Carol thought that discussions on how students arrived at their answers were threatening to take over all of her instructional time. Carol decided to use a weekly quiz to monitor student progress because she could see every student's work without taking away time from class. Anne asked Carol how quiz results were affecting her teaching, and Carol said that when most students failed an item on the quiz, she quickly reviewed the skill and repeated the item on the next week's quiz. Carol was frustrated and admitted that she thought formative assessment was simply too much additional time and effort.

Anne asked Carol if she wanted to see some formative assessment strategies that others had found successful. They agreed that Anne would teach Carol's class for several periods so that Carol could spend time observing other teachers who used formative assessments. To prepare for the observations, Carol returned to the *Self-Evaluation Record* and the *Formative Assessment Guide* to look at the guiding questions for Characteristic 2. She decided to focus on the question "How do you ensure that assessments are viable/feasible in the classroom?"

Following her observations, Carol interviewed the teachers about how they had time to include formative assessments in their class sessions. They agreed that the formative assessments changed the way in which they used their class time, but pointed out that they were able to gather information about student progress more frequently and adjust their lessons to ensure that students were not left behind as they moved through the unit. This practice took the place of doing continual remediation after each quiz, which also was time-consuming. One of the teachers talked about her strategy of pairing students to compare and discuss their problem-solving. In this way, the students could benefit from the thinking of others without requiring full class discussion. She said that students needed some guidance at first, but they quickly learned how to talk about their mathematics strategies.

Following the observations and discussions, Carol again met with Anne to develop a new plan for implementing this formative assessment approach. Carol liked the idea of treating the plan as an experiment in her class rather than as a major shift in how she taught. She decided to keep trying the whiteboard activity, but have students solve the problems on their whiteboards and then meet in groups of three or four to discuss their results and their problem-solving strategies. Seeing the range of responses on the whiteboards allowed Carol to target which students she wanted to be sure to listen to during this small-group work, and

(Continued)

(Continued)

sometimes she used the information to pair specific students together. Anne agreed to observe Carol at least weekly and to facilitate discussions among all the math teachers about their formative assessment practices.

This example illustrates the multiple ways in which a coach might help a teacher who is working to improve his or her formative assessment practices. As someone who was familiar with her instruction, Anne was able to encourage Carol to try some new practices. She facilitated other meetings with other teachers engaged in formative assessment. When Carol needed additional support to better understand how formative assessment could work practically for her, Anne taught for several class periods. Finally, Anne was able to provide ongoing support by observing Carol and facilitating continuing professional conversations among teachers in the school.

A Creative Scheduling Approach: A Role for a Principal

James, a principal in a K–3 elementary school, wanted to find time for teachers to meet in grade-specific learning communities. After-school meetings did not seem to be viable given existing teacher commitments, and the current schedule did not accommodate grade-alike teachers' meetings. He realized that while the teachers of "specials" (art, music, PE, technology) did not have homerooms, every other teacher did. Students met in their homeroom for approximately 40 minutes at the start of each school day, when they had sharing circles or addressed issues such as bullying. The time was important, but was not spent on formal curriculum learning.

Based on his reflection about the problem, James introduced some changes that only he, as principal, could make. Every Monday morning, the first-grade teachers met in a learning community while the teachers of the "specials" supervised their classes. On Tuesday mornings, the second-grade teachers met together, while again the teachers of the "specials" supervised their classes. The pattern was repeated on Wednesday and Thursday with the kindergarten and third-grade teachers. Then, on Fridays, the four "specials" teachers met in their own learning community. This pattern repeated every week. Thus, in the course of a month, teachers at each grade level and the "specials" had at least two hours of time in which to focus on aspects of formative assessment that were important to their specific group.

Introducing the change to the teachers required some sensitive handling, primarily for those teachers who taught "specials," since they essentially lost some free time. To address that issue, James engaged them in the discussion about the plan from the beginning, rather than imposing it. In addition, several mornings a month, he would bring all the students from a particular grade level together to meet with just him in the cafeteria; on those days the "specials" teachers benefited from the additional free time.

Summary: The Big Idea of Chapter 5

In this chapter, we focused on the act-reflect-revise cycle that is within the larger self-evaluation cycle. We also looked at specific sources of support for this process: learning communities, coaches, mentors, supervisors, and administrators. Each form of support plays out in a different way, but also offers opportunities for teachers to turn formative assessment plans into action and to give additional input to support their reflection on the implementation and support for the revision process.

Questions for Individual Consideration

1) How can you develop routines that help you find the time to complete the full act-reflect-revise cycle?

2) Who can provide support for you?

3) Who can you provide support for?

Questions for Consideration as a Learning Community

1) How can we support the act-reflect-revise cycle?

2) How can we provide support and accountability for each other?

3) What's our "weigh-in" routine?

6

Self-Evaluation of Changes to Practice

Earlier, we defined the distinctions among assessment, evaluation, and self-evaluation. Consistent with common classroom terminology, we use the term *assessment* when the focus is on student learning. We use *evaluation* or *self-evaluation* when the focus is on the effectiveness of your own practice. This book is all about self-evaluation, specifically in relation to formative assessment. In this chapter, we focus on self-evaluation of the changes you have made to your practice (the highlighted box in Figure 6.1). One way to think about it is that we want to help you answer these questions: "Was the change worth it?" or "Are the changes I made working? If not, why not?"

We begin this section with a concrete example to set the scene and in the following sections provide information you will need to document your formative assessment actions, logical and empirical linkages between actions and effects, and evidence of formative assessment effects on students. Systematically capturing sound evidence of change will enable you to see the nature and extent of your success and determine whether to move forward with new changes or revisit and improve your current formative assessment practices. Therefore, when you reach the end of this chapter, we want you to understand how to document your actions, consider key aspects of student effects for inclusion in your evidence collection, and effectively link your actions to student effects.

Figure 6.1 The Cycle-Within-the-Cycle Process: Evaluating Change

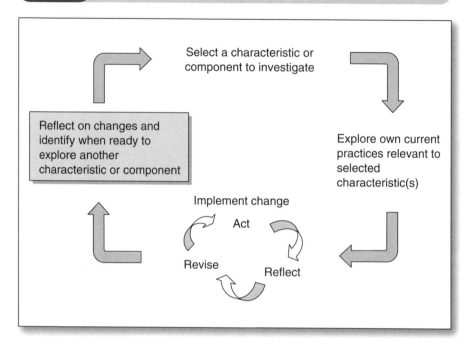

John teaches sixth-grade social studies. During a unit of study, he introduced students to the use of rubrics for several major projects for two reasons. First, he wanted to be clearer with his students about his learning expectations for them. Second, he wanted them to have a tool to use as they provided feedback to their peers. John had used the rubrics on a couple of occasions when students gave feedback to each other. Now he wanted to learn more about how they perceived that process.

At the end of a recent lesson, John gave students index cards and asked them to respond to two questions: What do you like most about getting feedback on your work from another student? What do you like least about getting feedback on your work from another student? In anticipation of his students' responses, he began to think about some possible struggles they might be having and ways he might address those struggles. He wondered, Do students understand the value of giving feedback to each other? Will they understand that they learn as they develop feedback for a peer? Do they know how to write feedback that is helpful?

Gaps between his expectations and student results provided points of focus for his analyses and follow-up. In his review of the responses, he formed groups of them by similar ideas, so he could see if there were common themes, both positive and negative, across the class, or blocks of outliers. The groups of most common, positive, and negative responses would then help him identify ways to improve his use of rubrics and student feedback. While the majority of students indicated that they found that comments from peers helped them improve their work, he noticed a small number of students commented that they did not like other students telling them what to do. John decided to spend part of a class period having a structured discussion with students about the kinds of comments that were helpful and not helpful and to review again why he was having them give feedback to each other (to help them think critically about their own work against the rubrics and to allow for more feedback to be shared than he could do on his own). Since the change he needed was relatively minor, John decided that he would move on to identify a new area of formative assessment to explore after he had the class discussion and students were able to continue to provide feedback.

Chain of Evidence

Most often your decisions about change (e.g., whether it was worth it) will not rest on a single event or assessment, as was the case with John's example. Rather, making sound decisions likely will rest on separate pieces of information that together lead toward a conclusion and course of action. In this text, we refer to the collection and assembly of such information as the creation of a chain of evidence. As the chain metaphor suggests, we anticipate that the respective pieces of gathered evidence will couple together to provide a chain or visible path. This chain leads from actions you took in planning and implementing formative assessment to judgments about its merit and worth—and actions that can further improve your work. When evaluating our formative assessment work, our chain will be composed of three types of links—evidence of formative assessment plans and actions, logical and empirical linkages between actions and effects, and evidence of formative assessment effects on students.

Documenting Formative Assessment Actions

In Chapter 4, we emphasized the importance of planning your actions to make changes in your formative assessment practice. Now, we want you to provide evidence to show either that you implemented your formative assessment practices as intended or that you adapted them as needed. (Every teacher knows that classes do not always go exactly, sometimes not even remotely, as planned.) Documenting your intended and actual actions is the first step to establishing relationships between your actions and their effects. Effects are only important insofar as they can be tied directly to what you did.

For example, say you chose to start with Characteristic 1, which calls for you to clearly state and share learning expectations with students. Keeping the lesson plans where you wrote out the learning expectations is good documentation, but not enough. To show the effect of your actions, you need to document what actually happened in the classroom. Good documentation of action would include other artifacts (e.g., handouts, sample entrance and exit tickets) and descriptions of what took place in the classroom (e.g., student questions about the learning expectations). The list below identifies other places to look for documentation of your formative assessment actions:

- Lesson plans
- Handouts
- Your descriptions of, reflections on, or notes about what happened in the classroom
- Videos or notes from peers or supervisors who observed your class
- Rubrics
- Student homework—for example, a case example of a student's work and feedback from you or his or her peers
- Quizzes and test scores

Keep in mind that feasibility is important here. Since you likely will not share your documentation of actions with others, it is probably sufficient to review the materials to ensure that you remember your actions correctly.

Finding Effects

Deciding where to look for the change you expect your actions to produce is the next step in self-evaluating your formative assessment practice. To save you some work on where to look for effects, we offer you a list from the National Staff Development Council report on teacher professional development (Killion, 2008). In it, Killion posited that teachers' professional development can be judged in terms of student effects in five areas: knowledge, attitude, skill, aspiration, and behavior. Within these five areas, you can look for student effects like improved content knowledge, more positive attitudes toward learning, more sophisticated disciplinary skills, increased aspirations for continued study, or changes in behavior. We offer further detail about how to collect evidence of effects later in this chapter. However, these five descriptors will help you set initial boundaries on what counts as evidence.

Linkages Between Actions and Effects

Now that you know there are many places to look for effects, you need to build linkages between your actions and the effects to prioritize your collection of evidence. As such, you will want to address and gather evidence only of effects that are clearly linked to your actions. For example, you might expect that there will be a logical connection between sharing learning expectations with your students and the knowledge they attain through the instructional process; therefore, knowledge would be an aspect in which you would want to collect evidence. To help you clarify the connection between actions and effects, we have included Table 6.1, a matrix that crosses Killion's (2008) effect areas with our four characteristics of formative assessment. This matrix of effect areas and formative assessment characteristics provides a complete picture of the actions, results, and linkages between them.

You can use the row, column, and cell characteristics of Table 6.1 to facilitate your determination of which evidence is most important to collect. For instance, you might be interested in evaluating the effects of your actions on student behavior. By reviewing the "Behavior" row, you can find or develop questions pertinent to actions for each of the formative assessment characteristics. If you address one formative assessment characteristic at a time, as we have encouraged, then you will want to pose questions in each effect area within that column. On any one given day, you likely will be most interested in a single cell of the table, the intersection between your characteristic of action and a particular expected effect.

We took the liberty of posing questions in each cell of Table 6.1 to give some general examples of how characteristic and the effect area can intersect. We intend those questions to help you consider the nature and extent of your evidence-collecting strategies. You may want to answer these questions in constructing a chain of evidence or develop other questions that better fit your particular situation. In Table 6.2, we offer an example that demonstrates how Susan (who in Chapter 4 decided to focus on using rubrics and exemplars as a way to make learning expectations more clear to students) used the linkages between characteristics and effects for her formative assessment work with learning expectations.

Table 6.1 Crossing Effect Areas With Formative Assessment Characteristics

Effect Areas[a]	Formative Assessment Characteristics			
	1	2	3	4
	Intended outcomes of learning and assessment are clearly stated and shared with students	Formative assessment opportunities are designed to collect quality evidence to inform teaching and improve learning	Formative feedback to improve learning is provided to each student	Students are engaged in the assessment process and, to the extent possible, in planning their own next steps for learning
Knowledge: Conceptual understanding of information, theories, principles, and research	What percentage of your students can demonstrate that they know the intended learning outcomes?	Do your assessments address retention of knowledge as well as acquisition?	Is your feedback timely and specific enough to guide student learning? Do you provide examples of good performance?	How does engaging students affect breadth and/or depth of learning?
Attitude: Beliefs about the value of particular information or strategies	Do your efforts to share learning objectives produce improved student attitudes toward learning?	Do students see the relevance of the assessment to their learning practices? Do students feel comfortable providing suggestions for improving the instruction setting?	What proportion of your students view formative feedback as helpful? Which types of feedback are better received by students and under what circumstances?	Do students value the opportunity to be actively involved in planning and conducting formative assessments?
Skill: The abilities to use strategies and processes to apply knowledge	Do you show students how the current learning situation (lesson) builds on ideas and information gained from previous lessons?	Are students provided criteria and templates to record their personal standing and learning progression for each learning topic?	Does your feedback change the students' ability to perform the learning tasks?	Have student capabilities to self-evaluate improved?

Effect Areas[a]	Formative Assessment Characteristics			
	1	2	3	4
	Intended outcomes of learning and assessment are clearly stated and shared with students	Formative assessment opportunities are designed to collect quality evidence to inform teaching and improve learning	Formative feedback to improve learning is provided to each student	Students are engaged in the assessment process and, to the extent possible, in planning their own next steps for learning
Aspiration: Desires or internal motivations to engage in a particular practice	Do students better aspire to learning the objectives when they fully understand them?	Do you gather data at times and in ways that encourage students to do better in their daily lessons and assignments?	Do you provide feedback to students from your formative assessments in timely ways that encourage students to do better in their daily lessons and assignments?	Do students demonstrate their interest in self-assessment and in collaborating with other students to assess their own work in efforts to improve learning?
Behavior: Consistent application of knowledge and skills	How does knowledge of the learning objective change students' approach to study and learning?	What proportion (none, few, half, most, all) of students do their best to provide you with sound information about their learning?	What evidence do you have that students are applying the feedback information in constructive ways?	Do students work together effectively or mess around more? Increase in sharing among students?

[a]Effect Areas descriptors are quoted from Killion (2008, p. 38)

Table 6.2	Susan's Questions for Self-Evaluation of Incorporating Learning Expectations

Formative Assessment Characteristic 1: Intended outcomes of learning and assessment are clearly stated and shared with students	
Effect Area	Susan's questions
Knowledge	How do you know that all students received and understood this message about intended outcomes?
Attitude	What evidence do you have that this knowledge affected student attitudes (e.g., increased their attention to the task at hand, increased interest)?
Skill	How do you know that the students appropriately applied their understanding of outcomes as they worked to achieve them? For example, did they apply criteria appropriately?
Aspiration	Did clarity about intended outcomes change their aspirations for completing the work?
Behavior	What effects did you see in terms of student behavior? For example, were they more intentional in their learning efforts?

We also have provided a blank matrix of the effect areas and characteristics in the associated web materials, Web Tool D. We encourage you to list specific evidence you will seek from students and others as you plan for gathering data in the matrix as well. If you also note the findings you obtain and the utility of those findings, your notes will provide you with concrete verification of your evidence chain and its use as well as feedback to improve your experience on your next round through the formative assessment cycle.

In the pages that follow, we present an array of suggested data collection strategies. As you read these examples, take time to relate those examples to Table 6.1. Note where specific strategies are focused in the table. Note, too, that some of these data collection tools gather information crossing cell and column lines. In some cases, an instrument may serve your evidence needs directly. In other cases, you will want to reformulate the instruments and strategies to limit them, to make them more feasible for your situation, or fine-tune them to better address points of interest to you.

Collecting Evidence of Effects

As we suggest with the questions in Table 6.1, you can collect a variety of types of evidence to examine your practice. Similarly, you can employ many strategies to gather that evidence. Neither the evidence nor the strategies are unique to formative assessment or even education. For example, someone who has taken up running might keep a journal and, for each run, record the distance covered and time taken. Reviewing those data after a couple of months can give a sense of improvement. Such logs are particularly valuable when the data are concrete and recorded in a systematic, easily accessible way. In the context of formative assessment, we think much of the evidence you will want to collect will go beyond what you can note in a journal or daily log.

The tools and approaches described in the following section are meant to extend and strengthen your reflections on practice. Often they will "validate" what you view as truth based on personal perceptions or anecdotal information obtained from students and others. At other times, the information gathered will run counter to your expectations. While confirming evidence is always welcome, we believe you will often find the counterevidence to be most beneficial. Such evidence will challenge you to look for alternative explanations and modify your approaches to make them stronger. Consider, for example, how useful a critical friend can be—one who provides carefully constructed, thoughtful analysis rather than simply agreeing with you. Such feedback may make you a bit uncomfortable, but that feedback makes it possible for you to change your instruction in ways that better serve student learning.

We know beginning the process can be challenging. Our own experience is that taking the first step is often the hardest. So, consider the next section of sources of information as a "starter kit" of tools and approaches. We chose them because they can be modified readily and adapted to meet your specific needs. The examples we present are categorized by two primary evidence sources: your students (through class work and observation) and peers (through their direct observation or audio/video recordings). Through all of these examples, we invite you to check the instruments against your chosen formative assessment characteristic and the specific student effects you are trying to achieve. Then tailor the individual tools and approaches in ways that best serve your personal formative assessment work.

Sources of Evidence

A variety of sources serve you in examining your formative assessment practices (McColskey & Egelson, 1997). What is most appropriate will depend on the characteristic on which you focused, the kinds of changes you have made and, being practical, how much time you have to collect evidence. Consider where and how you will collect evaluation information. Some may come from peers or others, some may be produced through observations or video recording, and some is stored in file drawers as reports of various forms. Most comes from the students. The list below touches on some of the sources noted in our formative assessment descriptions. Note the prominence of students in this list.

1. Student-generated information
    a. Direct feedback from students in the form of surveys or logs
    b. Indirect feedback from students in the form of student work, which could be tests, quizzes, homework, or in-class work samples
    c. Student-generated and student-summarized information about your instruction practices

2. Peer review
    a. Direct observation by a peer or a coach in the classroom
    b. Indirect observation using audio or video recordings reviewed after the lesson
    c. Review of documents by a peer

In the following subsections, we will address both of these sources of information in greater detail.

Student-Generated Information

Your students are an important source of feedback regarding changes that you have made in the classroom. Students spend at least six hours a day in school and certainly by middle school have formed opinions about teachers and teaching. Do not underestimate the value of what can be learned from them. Research cited by Airasian, Gullickson, Hahn, and Farland (1995) demonstrated that students can provide valid feedback as to the quality of instruction they have received. For example, students can provide feedback on the climate of the classroom and their perceptions of fairness. While you might think that you are extremely fair to students, if they perceive otherwise, that is an important piece of data to understand before you can begin to make changes.

It is possible that your students have never been asked for feedback before; you need to take that into consideration when you ask them for it. It is important that you provide students a context for the feedback and that you demonstrate as clearly as possible that the focus is on you, not them. Demonstrate this by soliciting anonymous feedback. You might even consider asking a student to collect the feedback—or depending on the age of your students—to summarize the feedback for you. To build trust, consider swapping classes with a peer when you administer a feedback tool. Each can administer a survey, you to your colleague's students and your colleague to yours. You can summarize the responses for your colleague's class and confirm the summary with the students before returning information to your colleague (and vice versa). This will let the students see that you are not giving their surveys to the other teacher, nor he or she to you.

Direct Feedback From Students

You can get direct feedback from students using a variety of methods and tools. One of the most straightforward is asking students for their perceptions of a formative assessment process you have incorporated into your teaching. Depending on the age of students, their reading ability, and what you are seeking feedback on, you also can use a variety of selected-response questions. You might ask them to respond to questions on a frequency scale (e.g., always, most of the time, sometimes, never) or to prompts on an agreement scale (e.g., strongly agree, agree, disagree, strongly disagree). You can make any of the scales simpler for your students (e.g., always, seldom, never; or agree, neither agree nor disagree, disagree). You are not necessarily aiming for a very precise measure; rather, you are looking to gain an overall sense of a single class or to learn about how perceptions might vary across classes. Keep the questions simple to prevent confusion. To take your use of direct feedback a step further, you can try to predict what your students' responses will be, as John did in the example at the beginning of this chapter.

Figures 6.2, 6.3, and 6.4 provide some starting points for your use in getting direct feedback from your students. These sets of questions are drawn from *The Teacher Self-Evaluation Tool Kit* (Airasian & Gullickson, 1997), and some questions in each figure have been added or revised to serve here. We have put these tools into our web-based resources to facilitate your use of them. Any of these questions and instruments can be modified for your own context; these are just examples to start your thinking.

Figure 6.2   Student Feedback on Formative Assessment

Student Feedback on Formative Assessment

Please answer honestly and do not put your name anywhere on this form.

1. How often does the teacher make clear what is expected of you in an assignment?
   a. Always
   b. Most of the time
   c. Sometimes
   d. Never

2. When you get something wrong on an assignment or test, how often does your teacher explain what you did wrong?
   a. Always
   b. Most of the time
   c. Sometimes
   d. Never

3. Does your teacher think it is important that every student in the class contribute to classroom discussion?
   a. Always
   b. Most of the time
   c. Sometimes
   d. Never

4. Does your teacher give you written comments on your work that help you figure out how to improve the work?
   a. Always
   b. Most of the time
   c. Sometimes
   d. Never

In Figure 6.2, we provide a series of questions that could be asked of students if you were seeking feedback about a variety of formative assessment approaches.

The questions included in Figure 6.3 address other aspects of formative assessment. Some of the questions could be modified to fit in other survey formats. Regardless of format, student anonymity is critical.

Our third example of how you might collect feedback from students is presented in Figure 6.4. Here, the focus is on more general issues of learning.

Figure 6.3 Student Feedback on Students Working Together

Student Feedback on Working Together

Please respond to each statement by circling "Agree" or "Disagree"		
1. Working with other students in class is helpful	Agree	Disagree
2. I am not always sure how to divide up work when we work in groups	Agree	Disagree
3. I like explaining my work to help another student	Agree	Disagree
4. I like having another student help me rather than the teacher	Agree	Disagree
5. Working in groups is difficult if one person does not try hard	Agree	Disagree
6. I like looking at other students' work to give them feedback	Agree	Disagree
7. I do not like other students looking at my work	Agree	Disagree
8. Others tease me when they review my work or provide me with feedback	Agree	Disagree

Figure 6.4 Student Feedback on Classroom Climate Issues

	3 Always True	2 Sometimes True	1 Never True
My teacher wants me to learn a lot	3	2	1
My teacher teaches me in many different ways	3	2	1
I learn lots of things in this class	3	2	1
My teacher believes that I can learn	3	2	1
My teacher helps me when I don't understand something	3	2	1
I believe that I can learn lots of new things	3	2	1
My teacher answers my questions	3	2	1
I can get smarter if I try hard	3	2	1

From the companion website you can download Web Tool E, which includes all three *Student Feedback Tools* found in Figures 6.2, 6.3 and 6.4.

For students who are a little older, you might decide to ask them more direct questions about specific aspects of formative assessment that you have introduced. Rather than asking them to complete an exit ticket based on the content of the lesson, you might ask them to respond to the question, "Why do you think I use an exit ticket at the end of the lesson? What do you think I do with your answers?" These sorts of questions address a common error teachers make—assuming that students understand your intent.

You may believe students understand that you collect information about critical learning from that day's lesson to help shape subsequent lessons. However, their understanding may differ significantly from your intentions. Collecting evidence of their understanding can either confirm that you were very transparent with the changes you made or that you need to provide some additional explanation to your students. One simple tool for checking quickly is called the one-minute assessment (Angelo & Cross, 1993). For example, when you believe you have presented the learning objective clearly and that all now understand it, stop and ask each student to jot down what to them was the muddiest point. Personal experience suggests the results will surprise you.

You might ask students why you ask them to participate in the development of criteria for judging outcomes, why you require them to give feedback to each other, or why you ask them to summarize key findings. Each has implications for types of change, knowledge, skills, attitudes, aspirations, and behaviors. Remember, the challenge is to develop a strand of evidence regarding some aspect or aspects of your formative evaluation practice. Cull items that do not directly focus on pertinent aspects, change items to make them fit better, and add items as needed.

As noted previously, with all these approaches to collecting evidence from students of the impact of changes to your practice, it is important to predict what their responses will be and then to compare your predictions with what they said. Significant differences between the two suggest areas for your attention.

Indirect Feedback From Students

The most commonly referenced indirect feedback from students occurs when teachers analyze student results from homework, quizzes, or tests to identify patterns of problems. For example, you might ask students to show their work when completing long-division arithmetic problems. You can choose one item from this homework and sort student responses on that item based on whether the work was fully correct or on the types of errors made in the process. Such analyses can be done quickly and have the benefit of sharpening your focus to see where instruction needs to be changed for the class as a whole. It also improves your insight into individual learning problems.

If the purpose of selecting a particular formative assessment characteristic to work on was to make an impact on student learning of a particular concept that students had historically struggled with, a source of evidence for the success of your efforts would be the student work generated after the implementation of the strategy. For example, you might decide to use exemplars to illustrate exactly what you mean by a quality lab report. Do the lab reports look significantly different this time around?

Student-Generated and Student-Summarized Information

Another less frequently considered facet of indirect feedback involves engaging students in developing information regarding your instruction, summarizing it, and providing results to you. This strategy engages students much like external observers would be used. When students serve as observers, the tasks must be carefully bounded, simple, and easily conducted with little or no distraction from the learning situation.

Consider the following strategy. From time to time, spice up your data collection efforts by engaging students to do the work and report findings to you. Suppose you want to improve your involvement with all students in your formative assessment practices. Perhaps you want to be sure that you are inclusive in calling on students. You might build criteria for yourself that goes something like the following. Each student must either pose a question or answer a question at least once every three days. You could prepare a check sheet and keep track as you lead discussion (this is difficult to do). Students probably will get into the spirit of your efforts if you engage them in the evaluative activity as well. You could assign one or two students to keep track for you and report back at the close of the three days. You could set up a strategy where students choose who will keep track, and you don't know who gathers the data or how, but you get summary information on how well you have met your goal. In one sense, these are simple counting exercises, not difficult to do, and perhaps a bit distracting for students who do the counting. On the other hand, it gives students a clear sense of how simple evaluations can play important roles in changing your behavior. That helps them see the relevance of such behaviors for their own practice.

Similarly, these strategies can be applied by groups of students and/or teams within your classroom. The point is that you do not have to be and should not be at the forefront of every data-gathering activity. Giving students responsibility for gathering and reporting data to you and to each other, along with authority to do this without interference from you, can enhance your evaluations. While giving these responsibilities to students can build their confidence, it also can overwhelm them or create divisiveness in the classroom. A little bit of authority and responsibility goes a long way. Start small, and incrementally increase both as students demonstrate their willingness and ability to properly engage. For students, it adds to the prestige and importance of the role assessment practices play in making decisions that serve and confirm sound instructional practices.

Peer Review

Other sources of information for the self-evaluation of your new formative assessment practice involve peers rather than students. You can invite individuals to observe you in the classroom or to watch a videotape of your instruction with you. They also can provide feedback on your documentation, like lesson plans, learning expectations, and questions. The following section describes some ways to make use of this resource.

Direct Observation With a Peer or Coach in the Classroom

Some of the guidance we gave in Chapter 4 about observing a peer to help you learn about formative assessment practices will still apply here—but in reverse. Now you are inviting a peer to come observe you and your classroom and to give you feedback on an aspect of *your* practice. When you observed a peer, you let that person know the specific focus of your observation. Likewise, when you invite someone to observe you for the purpose of giving you feedback, you want to give that person a focus. Let them know the specific area you have been working on with your students, and point to aspects for special attention. For example, suppose you are focused on Characteristic 3 regarding focused feedback. Here, you want to consider the impact of your feedback on student behavior. Provide context by sharing the nature and perhaps actual feedback information with the observer. Then ask the observer to classify student behavior in ways that serve your determination of impact. The observer might, for example, watch a random sample of students across several periods of time, each time determining whether the selected student was on or off task and, if on task, whether the student's behavior seemed to be related to feedback you provided to him or her.

Targeting the observer's focus simplifies the observation task and contributes to the usefulness of the information collected. The targeting also reduces the likelihood that the observation will result in generalities. General observation comments tend to have little relationship to your point of interest and decisions you must make to improve your instruction practices. Clear, specific information about your focus, on the other hand, can greatly improve your practice.

Indirect Observation Using Audio or
Video Recording Reviewed After the Lesson

What you look for and how you use this information parallels what was said about direct observations. New audio and video technology lets you skip around quickly and easily. This means you do not have to watch the whole video or audio recording. Rather, you can watch enough to get the context and then choose key snippets. Even the process you use to select segments to watch can be useful.

In focusing on this strategy, we again turned to examples found in Airasian and Gullickson (1997) and present them here as Figure 6.5. This strategy is aimed at identifying the nature and quality of the feedback teachers provide to students. Feedback may come in different forms for different assignments and subject areas, so this strategy may be employed usefully in more than one subject area or context (e.g., homework, tests, class discussion). Information to assess teacher feedback may be gathered by reviewing the comments on a set of student papers (reports, tests, drafts, and so on) after they have been graded or reviewed, by tape- or video recording a lesson, by asking students for feedback, or by having another teacher observe a lesson.

Again, we strongly encourage you to answer these questions for yourself before you begin to analyze student responses. For example, for Question 1, you might retrace your feedback patterns for the past two to three weeks and note your shortest, longest, and typical response times. Having actual times in hand as you read responses will help you confirm student perceptions, identify probable situations that students may see as problematic, and provide a basis for discussing your findings with your students.

Always, with this data collection tool and others described, return your findings (what your learned) to the students promptly after they answer your questions. Information sharing must flow in both directions—to you and back to students—if it is to become and remain a viable tool for evaluation purposes. Students soon weary of taking time to answer your questions if they do not see responses that serve their needs as well. Without your thoughtful responses to them, expect their responses to you to become perfunctory and hold little of value for you.

Figure 6.5   External Observer or Student Feedback Tool

External Observer or Student Feedback Tool

Please answer each question honestly.

1. How soon do I provide feedback on student papers and ideas?

2. How specific is the feedback? Do I use vague or general feedback like "good," "poor vocabulary," or "Work on this"? Or do I use specific feedback that informs the student like "good combination of adjectives to convey meaning"?

3. Do I focus feedback on specific behaviors or skills students can work on?

4. Do I show students how to perform correctly or give them examples of good performance?

5. Do I try to balance negative feedback with positive feedback?

6. Do I try to teach students to judge their own performances? Do I give them practice in doing this?

Once a teacher has a sense of his or her general practices in providing feedback, he or she can begin to consider whether these practices are consistent across various student groups (e.g., males-females, high ability–low ability, and so on.).

Figure 6.6 shows our modifications to the Figure 6.5 feedback tool for the purpose of determining how specific you are in the nature of feedback you provide. Perhaps your aim has been to increase the amount of specific feedback and reduce your use of general feedback. Choose a 10-minute span of time during the class period. For this time period, ask the observer to count the number of times you engage in each of these practices. If done as a video, the form can guide your analysis and check your in-class feedback to students. More effectively, ask a peer teacher to apply the form to your video.

Figure 6.6 Media Recording or External Observer Feedback Tool

---

Media Recording or External Observer Feedback Tool

1. Count (tally) the number of times I provide feedback during a 10-minute block of class. _____

2. How many different students received the feedback?
   _____

3. How specific is the feedback?
   a. Count the number of times I use vague or general feedback like "good," "poor vocabulary," or "Work on this." _____
   b. Count the number of times I use specific feedback that informs the student like "good combination of adjectives to convey meaning," show them how to perform correctly, or give them examples of good performance. _____

Note that Figure 6.6 has taken ideas from Figure 6.5, but has presented fewer of them in much more specific terms. Used this way, the observer does not judge your practice, but merely measures the frequency of your teaching feedback practices. These frequency counts require less judgment on the part of the observer and improve the reliability of the observation information.

Review of Documents by a Peer

When looking at specific documents, you might choose to ask a peer to think about your feedback, exit ticket questions, or learning intentions. Think through what role specific documents are intended to serve in your classroom and what outcomes are to be achieved through their use. Then develop questions that focus on those points along with strategies (e.g., sampling of student papers) that provide needed information for the review.

Note that ideas presented in Figure 6.5 serve these document review situations. They are easily applied to homework, test, and quiz situations. Have the peer teacher draw a "random" sample of papers (homework, for example) from a stack you have completed for return. Then choose one or two of the Figure 6.5 questions such as, "How specific is the feedback? Do I use vague or general feedback like "good," "poor vocabulary," or "Work on this"? Notice that Figure 6.6 can be modified quickly to serve this purpose.

Figure 6.7 is a variation on these ideas if you want to look more deeply at your teaching behaviors with different types of students.

Sampling student papers and selecting a few items for focus delimit the demands on the peer teacher and tend to focus the review process. Consider having the peer choose the item focus. That will keep you from focusing on what you think you do best. A variation of this would be to conduct the peer review of written feedback and then video the portion of the lesson during which you return student work, in order to also capture the associated class-based feedback that you provide.

Figure 6.7   Review of Student Work Tool

Review of Student Work Tool

Take the student papers (e.g., homework) and sort them into three piles. Include the best student work in the first pile, the typical or average student work in the second pile, and the poorest work in the third pile. Choose an equal number from each pile (e.g., five papers). For each student paper, use the form below to tally specifics about the feedback you provided.

Feedback Characteristic	Top Student Papers	Middle Student Papers	Bottom Student Papers
Total Amount of Feedback: Count the total number of times I provided feedback on this paper.	Student 1: _____ Student 2: _____ Student 3: _____ Student 4: _____ Student 5: _____ Total _____	Student 1: _____ Student 2: _____ Student 3: _____ Student 4: _____ Student 5: _____ Total _____	Student 1: _____ Student 2: _____ Student 3: _____ Student 4: _____ Student 5: _____ Total _____
Amount of General Feedback: Count the number of times I use vague or general feedback like "good," "poor vocabulary," or "Work on this."	Student 1: _____ Student 2: _____ Student 3: _____ Student 4: _____ Student 5: _____ Total _____	Student 1: _____ Student 2: _____ Student 3: _____ Student 4: _____ Student 5: _____ Total _____	Student 1: _____ Student 2: _____ Student 3: _____ Student 4: _____ Student 5: _____ Total _____
Amount of Specific Feedback: Count the number of times I use specific feedback that informs the student, like "good combination of adjectives to convey meaning," shows them how to perform correctly, or gives them examples of good performance.	Student 1: _____ Student 2: _____ Student 3: _____ Student 4: _____ Student 5: _____ Total _____	Student 1: _____ Student 2: _____ Student 3: _____ Student 4: _____ Student 5: _____ Total _____	Student 1: _____ Student 2: _____ Student 3: _____ Student 4: _____ Student 5: _____ Total _____

From the companion website you can download Web Tool F, which includes all three *Reviewer Tools* found in Figures 6.5, 6.6, and 6.7.

Our intention with this section was to illustrate some of the ways that you could structure the collection of evidence regarding the introduction of a new formative assessment practice into your classroom. You can directly or indirectly involve students in this process and also call on your peers to help you with the process. Across all the approaches, the important thing is to keep a clear focus on what exactly you—or a student or peer—are targeting. That will help you keep the data collection as streamlined and efficient as possible.

Additional Considerations

As you engage in data collection, a few additional issues should be considered: ownership and use of data, criteria for good data, and a common cause of weakness in an evidence chain.

Use of and Who Owns the Data

The evidence that you collect of student effects and changes in your classroom as a result of your formative assessment practice can serve multiple purposes, such as these:

- Direction for improvement and further refinement of your practice
- Continued self- and small-group reflection on formative assessment
- Mentoring other teachers in this particular kind of formative assessment
- Exemplars for others who want to develop evidence chains on the impact of their teaching
- Annual evaluations of your teaching with your principal
- School reporting about learning and other student outcomes
- Building confidence that your efforts made a difference

Keep in mind that you own the data collected for evaluation of your formative assessment practice. Therefore, you decide its uses and the extent to which it will be shared with others. For instance, it can be used as part of your annual personnel evaluation only if you decide to share it. In the rest of the chapter, we'll describe how to determine what evidence you need, how to collect it, and how to manage it. While we will suggest ways that your evaluation evidence can be used, determination of use rests securely in your hands.

Characteristics of Good Data

The characteristics of data we promote for this chain of evidence include these:

- Documentation—what you intended to do and what you actually did
- Based on criteria—focused on information about the change that is essential to understanding it
- Feasible to collect—data gathering fits into your schedule
- Boundaries—based on where you made changes or comparing with another class where you didn't make changes
- Clarity of relationships—create a clear picture of change by showing the causal links between the changes you made and the performance of your students
- Valid—your evidence is real, of good quality, and fairly represents your student effects
- Reliable—your measures provide consistent findings
- Proper—you acted fairly and appropriately in gathering data so that, for example, no harm comes to those who provide evidence to serve your evaluation

You cannot devote your full day to chasing down evidence. You must decide what information is essential and conduct your data gathering accordingly. Keeping your evidence-gathering tasks small helps to ensure that data gathering is feasible within your busy schedule.

A Common Cause of Weak Links in the Evidence Chain

We know that one common cause of weakness in an evidence chain is particularly important and pertains to self-interest. *The Student Evaluation Standards* (Joint Committee on Standards for Educational Evaluation, 2003) described it under the heading of conflict of interest. Conflict of interest can reduce the validity of evidence gathered. For example, a common behavior is to limit our evaluative probes to confirm our belief. You may ask a student or two if they understand the lesson objective. When you do that, and the two students provide reasonable answers, it is easy to assume that your instruction is supported by appropriate use of this formative assessment strategy. Perkins, Allen, and Hafner (cited in Airasian et al., 1995) refer to this as "my side" bias, "indicating that people tend to generate explanations that support their own point of view, to the exclusion of additional contradictory evidence" (p. 16). Test yourself. How often do you seek and sift through information to choose evidence that supports your position?

Summing Up

Through our examples, we have tried to show you data sources and strategies that you can apply in a variety of classroom settings to serve various aspects of your formative assessment development efforts. You may have noticed that Figures 6.5, 6.6, and 6.7 all address Characteristic 3 on feedback. Compare the items in those figures with Table 6.1, and you will note that not all aspects of Characteristic 3 are touched. Which ones are missed? Look again at the questions posed in conjunction with the five types of change. What questions might better serve your focus on Characteristic 3? Altogether, Figures 6.1 to 6.7 and other strategies we described can help you get started. Which ones are right for you and how are they best used? Those are decisions you must make.

  As a teacher, your role is to provide a learning path for your students to take them from unknowing or unskilled to knowing and skilled. In earlier chapters we have encouraged you to develop formative assessment practices that set student objectives, determine the gap between their current status and the intended objective, and effectively guide them to the objective. The chains of evidence ideas presented in this chapter pursue the same path. Here, however, you have to set the strategies for yourself. You determine the nature of information gathered, and you decide how findings are to be used to improve *your* skills. This is a substantial challenge for any teacher. We think the ultimate criterion of your success is when the evidence shows clearly that your students also do these same things for themselves.

Summary: The Big Idea of Chapter 6

In Chapter 4 we presented the idea of using data to examine your formative assessment practice and to select specific areas on which to focus. In that chapter, the data sources ranged from self-reflection on your own practices and descriptions and explanations of formative assessment to observations and interviews with colleagues. In this chapter we presented a series of additional sources of data and strategies that you can use to examine the question, "Were the changes worth it?" In this context, data sources ranged from student surveys and assessment evidence to peer observations, either directly in class or indirectly facilitated by audio or video recording.

Questions for Individual Consideration

1) Which tools presented in the chapter might be most useful to help you evaluate the impact of the changes you have been making to your practice?

2) Which characteristics are evident in Figure 6.2? Using the structure of Figure 6.2 and information provided in Table 6.1, how might you reconstruct items to focus solely on Characteristic 2?

3) Which form and strategy could you apply to assess student behavior in the context of Characteristic 4? What are the tradeoffs among two or three better strategies?

Questions for Consideration as a Learning Community

1) How can you help one another evaluate the impact of the changes you have been making in your classrooms?

2) What might you have to do in your school if you wanted to observe one another's classrooms?

3) What might you have to do in your school to find the time to evaluate feedback on student work or conduct other kinds of document reviews?

4) Look again at Table 6.2. What specifically could you do to gather evidence for the knowledge-level question Susan posed: "How do you know that all students received and understood this message about intended outcomes?

7

Putting It All Together

As you have read this book and used the tools presented in it and on the accompanying website, you have had the opportunity to learn more about formative assessment, examine your own teaching practice, work with colleagues who also are interested in formative assessment, and implement some new strategies in your own classroom. You have considered the impact of those changes in terms of student learning. You likely also made some decisions about the strategies you will use again and those you will set aside.

We hope that you return to the procedures outlined in this book as you continue to grow as a teacher. These processes can serve you in making changes to your practice, gaining support for those changes from peers and others within your school, and evaluating the worth of those changes in order to refine them as needed. This chapter briefly summarizes the major ideas we presented and provides some reminders to consider as you continue your professional growth in the use of formative assessment.

The early chapters of this book emphasized the basis of formative assessment and its benefits for student learning. Formative assessment is the continuous process in which students and teachers engage to monitor learning and to inform future instruction. We distinguished between formative assessment, with its emphasis on students, and evaluation, which emphasizes teachers examining and improving their practice. Table 1.1 (in Chapter 1) highlights the differences between these two ideas as they are presented and discussed in this book.

Throughout the book, we have emphasized that self-evaluation is a cyclical process (see Figure 7.1). Specifically, it offers you the opportunity to reflect on your practice, select an area to improve, put your changes into practice, analyze the results, revise, and try again. This process focuses on your learning goals as a teacher. As you work to improve your use of formative assessment practices, you will be asking these questions continually: Where am I going? Where am I now? How do I close the gap?

Figure 7.1 The Cycle-Within-the-Cycle Process: Narrowing Your Focus

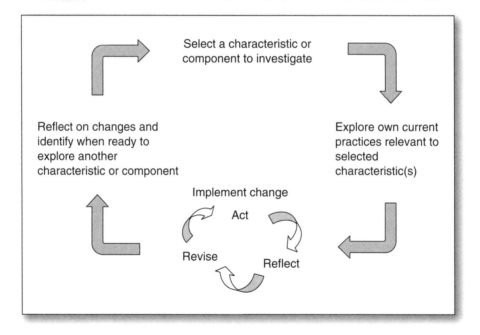

Teachers and students will use a variety of approaches to get information about whether individual students are making progress toward learning expectations. This information should be gathered frequently and then used to adjust instruction. Adjustments can take the form of feedback, peer support, and/or new or adapted instruction. We suggested four characteristics of formative assessment to help organize your professional development process. The *Formative Assessment Guide* lists each characteristic and provides examples of the characteristic in practice.

Four Characteristics of Formative Assessment

1. Intended outcomes of learning and assessment are clearly stated and shared with students.

2. Formative assessment opportunities are designed to collect quality evidence that informs teaching and improves learning.

3. Formative feedback to improve learning is provided to each student.

4. Students are engaged in the assessment process and, to the extent possible, in planning their own next steps for learning.

Characteristic 1 focuses on the teachers' role to make learning goals clear to students through the use of learning expectations (what students are to know and understand) and success criteria (what students will be able to do). Both learning expectations and success criteria should be based on relevant standards, curriculum guides, and student needs, and offer a trajectory of student learning. Learning expectations are shared with students on a daily basis in language they can understand. What constitutes successful and quality work (and success criteria) is described in age-appropriate language and discussed with students frequently.

The second characteristic of formative assessment—formative assessment opportunities are designed to collect quality evidence that informs teaching and improves learning—addresses how teachers can elicit evidence of student learning at different stages in instruction: at the launch of learning, during instruction, and at the close of learning. Teachers can use informal and formal preassessments at the start of a lesson or unit of study to inform the development of an instructional plan that meets the needs of all students. Both teachers and students can use formative assessment practices throughout the course of a unit to monitor progress and understanding. Finally, teachers can use evidence from summative assessments to identify students who may need further support. Teachers can use the information to consider how to adapt future instructional units to meet those needs.

Because usefulness of formative assessment depends on the quality of information collected, attention must be given to quality at every stage. This includes the creation of questions—whether a brief question at the end of the lesson, a discussion prompt, or a more involved task. Issues related to the questions, prompts, or tasks themselves include these: Does it address the learning expectation? Is it clear? Is it comprehensive enough for the intended purpose? Quality also pertains to other factors. Two especially important factors are whether the information gathered is sufficiently representative of the class and special groups of students and whether the information is gathered and used in a timely way.

Characteristic 3 focuses on the use of formative feedback to support student learning. Formative feedback focuses on helping students understand where they are in their current learning, where the teacher wants them to be, and how they can move forward. The feedback is tied directly to the learning expectations, and strengths and weaknesses are explained to the students. For feedback to be considered truly formative, students must have both time (opportunity) and guided structure to apply the feedback to the current piece of work.

The final characteristic of formative assessment addresses the role of students: students are engaged in the assessment process and, to the extent possible, in planning their own next steps for learning. There are two components to this theme: students' self-evaluation of their own work and learning and peer assessment of work. In both instances, teachers need to model the processes involved and ensure that students have access to a variety of self-evaluation and peer-assessment tools. The results of student feedback are never used for summative purposes.

With the four characteristics of formative assessment in hand, Chapter 3 addressed how to select a starting point for engaging in formative assessment. We presented three ways that you might expand your own knowledge of formative assessment and your understanding of how your current practice lines up with what is described in the research literature. We suggested that you work through the *Formative Assessment Practices Survey* as a way of thinking about your practice. We also suggested talking with colleagues and reflecting on your practice. We asked you to identify an area of focus for examining your practice in much more detail. We noted that the entire self-evaluation process is cyclical, so you may come back to this point repeatedly as you are ready to take on a new challenge.

Having selected one of the characteristics to consider, in Chapter 4 we asked you to engage in more detailed investigation by self-evaluation and by collecting data about exemplary practice related to that characteristic. We encouraged data collection through interviews with colleagues, classroom observations, or document reviews. We also encouraged you to use the *Self-Evaluation Record* for support and guidance as you moved through this process. At the conclusion of Chapter 4, you developed a plan for trying some new strategies in your classroom.

Changing formative assessment practice takes time and support. In Chapter 5 we reviewed the act-reflect-revise cycle and considered the variety of people who can provide support and accountability as you engage in this cycle. We discussed three potential sources of support: a coach, a learning community, and a building administrator who serves as an instructional leader. Although it is certainly possible to work on improving your formative assessment practices on your own, we encourage you to seek out the support structures that will help you sustain your efforts.

Finally, in Chapter 6, we discussed a series of additional sources of data and strategies you can use to evaluate the effects of your formative assessment practices. The question examined most prominently was, "Were the changes worth it?" In this context, data sources ranged from student surveys and assessment evidence to peer observations, either directly in class or indirectly, facilitated by audio or video recording. We recognize that you and your colleagues will want to know that the efforts you are making to implement formative assessment practices are making a positive difference for your students. Where your efforts fall short of your objectives, the evaluation information can help you identify ways to improve these practices.

We hope that you complete the entire process of self-evaluation multiple times. As you complete your first cycle of self-evaluation (reflecting on your practice, selecting an area for improvement, putting your changes into practice, analyzing the results, and revising again), you may ask yourself how you will know it is time to move on to a new target. First, your new formative assessment strategy should seem like a habit before you try something else. Second, you should be experiencing some success with your new strategy related to student learning. If the formative assessment practice has become a habit and you obtain successful results, you now have a foundation to select and build in new practices. You may find that starting a new semester or school year with a new group of students brings new challenges—things that work with one set of students may not be as successful with another. Importantly, the reverse is also true. Something that was not successful with one group of students may be worth trying again with a new group of students. The second time around, you might approach it a little differently, explain it differently, or just be a little more experienced yourself, and find that it is a useful tool.

Throughout this book, we have provided examples of how teachers have enacted the formative assessment process in their classrooms in ongoing ways. And yet these examples cannot fully represent the breadth of practice that thoughtful and creative teachers have brought to the formative assessment process. While we have drawn on examples from a range of content areas and grade levels, there are also many gaps. We have not had the space to illustrate specifically how special education or teachers of students for whom English is not their first language have incorporated formative assessment into their teaching.

We encourage all teachers to consider how greater clarity and explicitness of learning outcomes might help their students. We also encourage all teachers to develop new ways to understand what and how students are learning. These new ways can help stretch students that need greater challenges and provide additional support for those who are struggling.

Regardless of content area, we encourage all teachers to think about how they could provide feedback to students to help their understanding. This feedback should not only inform them when they have not yet met the learning outcomes, but also provide direction and actions for improvement. Finally, even where we have not been able to illustrate exactly what it can look like, we encourage all teachers to develop ways to use students as resources for each other to support the learning of their peers.

As we have clearly advocated, the challenges of applying research to the classroom are best confronted with a support structure. Answers to difficult questions and determination to persist when times are difficult often flow from the wisdom and practice of other colleagues. When, how, and in what ways you can draw upon colleagues will differ from individual to individual and from school to school. We believe it is worth your investment in time and effort to identify or build such structures.

Some of the best ideas for formative assessment may not neatly fit your teaching situation. When examples do not directly apply to your teaching context, take time to consider the practice against the four characteristics of formative assessment. This will help you better understand the character and spirit of each one. From there, you can then ask, what would it look like in my teaching context? And as you try out new approaches, you can again hold them up to the four characteristics to ask yourself whether your actions are true to those principles.

Finally, as you share formative assessment practices with other teachers, remember that formative assessment is for everyone—from beginning teachers to seasoned veterans. The formative process can help teachers who struggle with instruction to those who excel in the classroom. As in other professions, learning does not stop once an individual receives a degree and a license to practice. Professional learning is a career-long process.

We wish you well on your formative assessment journey. Formative assessment is a powerful tool that can improve teacher practice on a continuous basis if implemented properly and consistently. In turn, it can increase student interest, motivation, and learning. Implement formative assessment with fidelity, enjoy its fruits in your classroom, and spread the word about its positive impact on teachers and students alike.

References

Airasian, P. W., & Gullickson, A. R. (1997). *The teacher self-evaluation tool kit.* Thousand Oaks, CA: Corwin.

Airasian, P. W., Gullickson, A. R., Hahn, L., & Farland, D. (1995). *Teacher self-evaluation: The literature in perspective.* Kalamazoo: The Evaluation Center, Western Michigan University.

Andrade, H. L., & Cizek, G. J. (Eds.). (2010). *Handbook of formative assessment.* New York: Routledge.

Angelo, T. A., & Cross, K. P. (1993). *Classroom assessment techniques: A handbook for college teachers.* San Francisco: Jossey-Bass.

Bergan, J. R., Sladeczek, I. E., & Schwarz, R. D. (1991). Effects of a measurement and planning system on kindergartners' cognitive development and educational programming. *American Educational Research Journal, 28*(3), 683–714.

Black, P., Harrison, C., Lee, C., Marshall, B., & Wiliam, D. (2003). *Assessment for learning: Putting it into practice.* Buckingham, UK: Open University Press.

Black, P. J., & Wiliam, D. (1998). Assessment and classroom learning. *Assessment in Education: Principles, Policy and Practice, 5*(1), 7–73.

Boyd, D., Grossman, P., Ing, M., Lankford, H., Loeb, S., & Wyckoff, J. (2011). The influence of school administrators on teacher retention decisions. *American Educational Research Journal, 48.*

Brookhart, S. M. (2005). *Research on formative classroom assessment.* Paper presented at the Formative Classroom Assessment: Research, Theory, and Practice symposium. Annual meeting of the American Educational Research Association, Montreal.

Butler, R. (1987). Task-involving and ego-involving properties of evaluation: Effects of different feedback conditions on motivational perceptions, interest, and performance. *Journal of Educational Psychology, 79,* 474–482.

Butler, R. (1988). Enhancing and undermining intrinsic motivation: The effects of task-involving and ego-involving evaluation of interest and performance. *British Journal of Educational Psychology, 58*(1), 1–14.

Carpenter, T. P., Fennema, E., Peterson, P. L., Chiang, C., & Loef, M. (1989). Using knowledge of children's mathematics thinking in classroom teaching: An experimental study. *American Educational Research Journal, 26*(4), 499–531.

Council of Chief State School Officers. (2008). *Formative assessment: Examples of practice.* A work product initiated and led by Caroline Wylie, ETS, for the Formative Assessment for Students and Teachers (FAST) Collaborative. Washington, DC: Author.

Crooks, T. (1988). The impact of classroom evaluation practices on students. *Review of Educational Research, 58*(4), 438–481.

Darling-Hammond, L., Wei, R. C., Andree, A., Richardson, N., & Orphanos, S. (2009). *Professional learning in the learning profession: A status report on teacher development in the United States and abroad.* Stanford University: National Staff Development Council and the School Redesign Network.

Day, J. D., & Cordon, L. A. (1993). Static and dynamic measures of ability: An experimental comparison. *Journal of Educational Psychology, 85*(1), 75–82.

DuFour, R. (2004). Schools as learning communities. *Educational Leadership, 61*(8), 6–11.

Educational Testing Service. (2009). *TLC leader handbook.* Portland, OR: Author.

Fontana, D., & Fernandes, M. (1994). Improvements in mathematics performance as a consequence of self-assessment in Portuguese primary school pupils. *British Journal* of *Educational Psychology, 64*(3), 407–417.

Fuchs, L. S., Fuchs, D., Karns, K., Hamlett, C. L., Dutka, S., & Katzaroff, M. (2000). The importance of providing background information on the structure and scoring of performance assessments. *Applied Measurement in Education, 13*(1), 1–34.

Glickman, C., Gordon, S., & Ross-Gordon, J. (2009). *Supervision and instructional leadership: A developmental approach.* Boston: Allyn and Bacon.

Hallinger, P., & Heck, R. H. (1998). Exploring the principal's contribution to school effectiveness: 1980–1995. *School Effectiveness and School Improvement: An International Journal of Research, Policy and Practice, 9*(2), 157–191.

Hattie, J. (2009). *Visible learning; A synthesis of over 800 meta-analyses relating to achievement.* London: Routledge.

Hattie, J., & Timperley, H. (2007). The power of feedback. *Review of Educational Research, 77*(1), 81–112.

Heritage, M. H. (2010). *Formative assessment: Making it happen in the classroom.* Thousand Oaks, CA: Corwin.

Joint Committee on Standards for Educational Evaluation. (2003). *The student evaluation standards.* Thousand Oaks, CA: Sage.

Killion, J. (2008). *Assessing impact* (2nd ed.). Thousand Oaks, CA: Corwin.

King, A. (1992). Facilitating elaborative learning through guided student-generated questioning. *Educational Psychologist, 27*(1), 111–126.

Kluger, A. N., & DeNisi, A. (1996). The effects of feedback interventions on performance: A historical review, a meta-analysis, and a preliminary feedback intervention theory. *Psychological Bulletin, 119*(2), 254–284.

Knight, J. (2005). A primer on instructional coaches. *Principal Leadership, 5*(9), 6–21.

Lally, P., van Jaarsveld, C. H. M., Potts, H. W. W., & Wardle, J. (2010, October). How are habits formed: Modeling habit formation in the real world. *European Journal of Social Psychology, 40*(6). http://onlinelibrary.wiley.com/doi/10.1002/ejsp.674/full.

Marzano, R. J., Waters, T., McNulty, B. A. (2005). *School leadership that works: From research to results.* Alexandria, VA: Association for Supervision and Curriculum Development.

McColskey, W., & Egelson, P. (1997). *Designing teacher evaluation systems that support professional growth.* Tallahassee, FL: SERVE.

McManus, S., & Council of Chief State School Officers. (2008). *Attributes of effective formative assessment.* A work product coordinated and led by Sarah McManus, North Carolina Department of Public Instruction, for the Formative Assessment for Students and Teachers (FAST) Collaborative. Washington, DC: Council of Chief State School Officers.

Mercer, N., Wegerif, R., & Dawes, L. (1999). Children's talk and the development of reasoning in the classroom. *British Educational Research Journal, 25*(1), 95–111.

Natriello, G. (1987). The impact of evaluation processes on students. *Educational Psychologist, 22,* 155–175.

Nyquist, J. B. (2003). *The benefits of reconstructing feedback as a larger system of formative assessment: A meta-analysis.* Unpublished master's thesis. Vanderbilt University, Nashville, TN.

Popham, W. J. (2008). *Transformative assessment.* Alexandria, VA: Association for Supervision and Curriculum Development.

Quinn, D. M. (2002). The impact of principal leadership behaviors on instructional practice and student engagement. *Journal of Educational Administration, 40*(5), 447–467.

Sadler, R. (1989). Formative assessment and the design of instructional systems. *Instructional Science, 18,* 119–124.

Schon, D. (1983). *The reflective practitioner.* London: Temple Smith.

Simmons, M., & Cope, P. (1993). Angle and rotation: Effects of different types of feedback on the quality of response. *Educational Studies in Mathematics, 24*(2), 163–176.

Thompson, M., & Wiliam, D. (2008). Tight but loose: A conceptual framework for scaling up school reforms. In E. C. Wylie (Ed.), *Tight but loose: Scaling up teacher professional development in diverse contexts* (RR-08-29, pp. 1–44). Princeton, NJ: Educational Testing Service.

White, B. Y., & Frederiksen, J. R. (1998). Inquiry, modeling, and metacognition. Making science accessible to all students. *Cognition and Instruction, 16*(1), 3–118.

Wiliam, D. (2004, June). *Keeping learning on track: Integrating assessment with instruction.* Presented at the 30th International Association for Educational Assessment Conference, Philadelphia.

Wiliam, D., Lee, C., Harrison, C., & Black, P. (2004). Teachers developing assessment for learning: Impact on student achievement. *Assessment in Education, 11*(1), 49–65.

Wylie, C., & Lyon, C. (2009, August). What schools and districts need to know to support teachers' use of formative assessment. *Teachers College Record.*

Index

f or *t* after a page number indicates a figure or table.

CORWIN

A SAGE Company

The Corwin logo—a raven striding across an open book—represents the union of courage and learning. Corwin is committed to improving education for all learners by publishing books and other professional development resources for those serving the field of PreK–12 education. By providing practical, hands-on materials, Corwin continues to carry out the promise of its motto: **"Helping Educators Do Their Work Better."**